CREATIVE PREACHING

Abingdon Preacher's Library

Liberation Preaching, Justo L. and Catherine G. González
The Person in the Pulpit, Willard F. Jabusch
The Preaching Moment, Charles L. Bartow
Designing the Sermon, James Earl Massey
The Preaching Tradition, DeWitte T. Holland
The Sermon as God's Word, Robert W. Duke
Creative Preaching, Elizabeth Achtemeier
The Word in Worship, William Skudlarek
Preaching as Communication, Myron R. Chartier
A Theology of Preaching, Richard Lischer
Preaching Biblically, William D. Thompson

CREATIVE PREACHING
Finding the Words

Elizabeth Achtemeier

Abingdon Preacher's Library

William D. Thompson, Editor

ABINGDON
Nashville

Creative Preaching: Finding the Words

Copyright © 1980 by Abingdon

Second Printing 1981

All rights reserved.

Library of Congress Cataloging in Publication Data

ACHTEMEIER, ELIZABETH RICE, 1926–
  Creative preaching.
  (Abingdon preacher's library)
  Bibliography: p.
  Includes index.
  1. Preaching. 2. Creation (Literary, Artistic, etc.)
  I. Title.
  BV4211.2.A27   251.   80-16890

ISBN 0-687-09831-9 (pbk.)

MANUFACTURED BY THE PARTHENON PRESS AT NASHVILLE, TENNESSEE, UNITED STATES OF AMERICA

In memory of my mother,
Ida Schafer Rice,
faithful steward,
who listened to the Word of God
and kept it
and passed it on

CONTENTS

EDITOR'S FOREWORD

Preaching has captured the attention of increasingly large segments of the American public. Lay parish committees seeking pastoral leadership consistently rank preaching as the most desirable pastoral skill. Seminary courses and clergy conferences on preaching attract participants in larger numbers than ever. Millions of viewers watch television preachers every week.

What is *good* preaching? is the question of both those who hear it and those who do it. Hearers answer that question instinctively, tuning in the preacher who meets their needs, whether in the pulpit of the neighborhood church or on a broadcast. Preachers need to answer more intentionally.

Time was that a good thick book on preaching would do it, or a miscellaneous smattering of thin ones. The time now seems ripe for a different kind of resource—a carefully conceived, tightly edited series of books whose scope covers the homiletical spectrum and whose individual volumes reveal the latest and best thinking about each specialty within the field of preaching. The volumes in the Abingdon Preacher's Library enable the preacher to understand preaching in its historical setting; to examine its biblical and theological underpinnings; to explore its spiritual, relational, and liturgical dimensions; and to develop insights into its craftsmanship.

Designed primarily for use in the seminary classroom, this series will also serve the practicing preacher whose background in homiletics is spotty or out-of-date, or whose preaching needs strengthening in some specific area.

William D. Thompson
Eastern Baptist Theological Seminary
Philadelphia, Pennsylvania

I. CREATIVITY AND AUTHORITY

Creativity in the pulpit is not a matter of continually coming up with new and different sermon ideas or of preaching from obscure texts never heard before by the congregation. It does not consist of surprising one's people with a striking sermon form or of scandalizing them with coarse or colloquial language. Above all, creativity in the pulpit is not a matter of manipulating a congregation with emotional tales or of delighting them with their preacher's cleverness and ingenuity. No preacher can show forth simultaneously his or her own cleverness and the lordship of Jesus Christ.

No, a preacher may deal with a well-known text within a standard three-point outline, deliver the sermon in the most quiet and unspectacular fashion, and still be creative. For creative preaching is the fashioning of a sermon into such an artistic and effective whole that the Word of God, spoken through the text, is allowed to create that reality of which it speaks within the individual and corporate lives of the gathered congregation. Creative preaching is the release of the active Word of God to do its judging and saving work. Creative preaching is the medium of the working of a present God within the lives of his people on any given Sunday morning. In short, creative preaching is creative because it is the tool of the creative and re-creating God. Its effectiveness comes not from itself but from the Lord whom it serves. Its power is not that of its own words, but of the lively Word of the Lord.

11

WHY CREATIVITY?

Since that is the case, we might ask why it is necessary to labor over our sermons at all. Surely the powerful Word of God needs no help from us! There was once a student in homiletics class who, in a mistaken interpretation of Barthian theology, thought it sufficient simply to dump on the congregation the full meaning of the text at the beginning of the sermon. From that point on, she reasoned, the Word of God would do its work, and her sermon could then end with only a few admonitions to hear and apply the Word. And it is testimony to the power of the Word that occasionally such a method has worked. The great preacher Charles Haddon Spurgeon told of being converted by a preacher who, lacking anything else to say, constantly repeated his text. The smouldering Word of God burned deeply into Spurgeon's heart and burst into unquenchable evangelical flame. But that does not happen very often. It has pleased God, said the apostle Paul, through the folly of the message we preach, to save those who believe—to set between the Word and the world the figure of the preacher; to entrust the incomparable riches of Christ to the earthen containers of our human words. Perhaps the reason is that only in that way can a congregation inherit and live from the gospel's wealth.

The Word of God, incarnate in Christ, has been handed down to the church in the form of the confessions of faith known to us as the biblical record. That record is thick with history: the rise and fall of empires; the ups and downs of the nation called Israel; the miseries and glories of countless individual lives. At the same time, it is fluid with constantly shifting interpretations of tradition and event and doctrine; with additions to and subtractions from the text; with redactions and rearrangements of material; with changing forms and altered emphases and new inserted inspirations. And out of this deposit of actual human life, there comes the testimony: This is who God is, and this is what he has done in our experience.

To sort out all that—to master the history, to trace the reinterpretations, to identify the forms, to see the emphases in the new redactions, to translate the ancient world-views in order that the testimony may be clearly heard and the meaning fully understood—that is the task of the preacher, the interpreter of the Word of God to the people. No congregation can handle the task fully, on its own. The biblical record may be so strange to a congregation that it seems to be a message from another planet. The preacher has the creative task of making it clear in his or her particular parish.

It is not sufficient, however, simply to elucidate the meaning of a biblical passage. An explained text still may remain a dead and distant word from the past, having apparently nothing to say to the listening congregation. The point is, What difference does the Word make? Is there anything at stake in the text for the people in the pews? Will the biblical Word re-create their lives? Here the mediation of the preacher plays a vital role.

We often preach in the church to persons who are sure that they are Christians; for whom there hangs over the biblical record what Fred Craddock has called "the dead air of familiarity"; for whom attendance at worship is habitual routine, and the Christian way of life synonymous with the life-style to which they have become accustomed. The task of the preacher then is to sharpen the hearing of those whose ears have been dulled by the feeling of having heard it all before. For such persons, there are accustomed subjects with which preachers deal, familiar ways in which things religious are treated. The preacher has the task of so utilizing language that the newness of the text comes shining through, and God's act of which the text speaks is done astoundingly afresh among the listeners.

In our age we also preach in the church, and outside it, to persons who have lost all credence in words. The average American is daily bombarded with words—words intended to make us buy, to make us believe, to make us do. Our lives are constantly manipulated by words, and perhaps fortunately for our personal freedom, we have become rather cynical about all words. Words are nothing but propaganda or advertisement, we think, or words are little more than public relations gimmicks, intended to create an image. The preacher therefore has the task of speaking words in such a fashion that they are not just more sounds added to the slick sales pitches of producers and some politicians, but are perceived by the congregation actually to speak the truth in love.

Indeed, in our age a preacher's language must be so fashioned that the very act of hearing regains credibility, for we are addressing a generation accustomed to acting primarily on visual stimuli. The picture on the billboard, the image on the TV screen, the visual effects of the newest movie—these are the symbols that capture the modern imagination. Color, light, action, but also texture and scent, taste and speed—these form the ambience of our life. We live and move and have our being in a world of soft fabrics and eye-catching colors, of fizzing drinks and dizzying rides, of flashing signs and perfumed aromas—in short, in a world which seeks to stimulate every one of our senses. And yet we preach a God who demands primarily that we hear. The Christian ethic is an ethic of the ear and not of the eye or touch or taste or smell. In our modern age the preacher must therefore translate the biblical message into one that awakens all the senses, into words that cause a congregation also to see and feel and smell and taste. Otherwise the listening people may never hear the words in which the gospel is framed.

More seriously still, we are addressing a generation of persons who see few new possibilities for themselves. Many of them have some dreadful sense of isolation and loneliness—the unease that no human relationship is just quite right, but that all are quirked with misunderstandings and little wounds inflicted and empty words that have lost the power to convey anything of their hearts.

Many of our people know a terrible joylessness—the fact that every thrill has been worn threadbare now and that they can no longer have a good time just because they want to. In Robert Frost's words,

> Now no joy but lacks salt,
> That is not dashed with pain
> And weariness and fault.[1]

Many also have the feeling of utter helplessness—the sense of vast wheels turning: of governments and terrorists, of bureaucracies and wars, of economics and multinational organizations, which determine how they live and die and how painful it shall be—and the feeling that no individual can do a single thing about it.

We address a people of almost total moral confusion, who on the fringes of their lives constantly must manage and mask adulteries and alcoholism and addictions. We live in a society in which bribery is a way of business and government, in which default on loans is an accepted standard for college students, in which fraud in what we say and think, in how we dress and entertain, is a recognized way to climb the social ladder. Many among us no longer know what is right or wrong. Others have become the slaves of forces that do not really care. As with Jeb Magruder of Watergate fame, somewhere between their ideals and their ambitions, they lose their moral compass, and so,

> Alone, alone, about a dreadful wood
> Of conscious evil runs a lost mankind.[2]

absurdity of gospel

Over against that lostness, in the midst of this society that sees no hope for itself; to persons who are sure that no good thing, lovely and pure and gracious, can endure and who are therefore certain that the high morning road of faith's pilgrimage is not for them, we preachers bring the announcement that a New Age, with new possibilities, has dawned. The kingdom of God has broken into human life in the person of Jesus Christ, and now every human love can find its healing, and every life its compass. The tyranny of nations and fate, of historical and natural forces, is now subject to the rule of that God who is uniting all things in his Son. Behind every personal history there can be meaning and the goodly power of a guiding God. The possibility for all is now one of joy and purpose, of new beginning and blessed outcome in a New Community. But to make our people see the New Age in their midst, to allow them to picture it and experience it and know it, we preachers must summon words that will enable "old men to dream dreams" and "young men to see visions"; that will enable our congregations to experience that reality they have rarely experienced before—the reality of human life permeated by and totally subject to the loving rule of a sovereign God.

"God chose what is foolish in the world to shame the wise, God chose what is weak in the world to shame the strong" (I Cor. 1:27). He has chosen us preachers so to exercise our creativity in his service that our people will know through our mortal words his immortal presence working in their midst. For that reason, above all others, we need to labor over our words, for we finally are given the task of making known the active person of the living God, in the midst of his gathered people.

 LABOR over OUR WORDS

What words can we borrow to encompass his glory? We can tell what he has done in the past, as assurance of what he is doing now: how his love in Jesus Christ brought forth trees and lakes and waterfalls, scarlet tanagers and pink coral reefs and white daisies along the road; how his care marks the flight and fall of each sparrow and numbers the hairs of our heads; how his faithfulness brings the round of "seedtime and harvest, cold and heat, summer and winter, day and night"; how his laughter produced the hippopotamus and giraffe and walrus and lumbering tortoise.

We can tell of God's might: how he flung galaxies across the darkness of space and centered energy in black holes in the sky, or how he gathered up the storm in his hands and packed it into an atom.

We can recall the Lord's humility when he bothered to go into Egypt to join forces with a bunch of half-civilized slaves who were making bricks with straw. We can tell how he grieved and loved and labored over his adopted son called Israel, and how he wept when he saw that he would have to hand his people over to the petty empires that would despoil them.

We can relate the amazing story of a maiden called Mary, overshadowed by his power; and of a stable-cave in the city of David; and of a carpenter's shop in Nazareth; and then of a Man who called him "Father" and who set out to find God's lost children, entering into the loneliness and pain and suffering of every wandering son and daughter, and finally carrying their evil burdens and dying their deserved deaths.

And yes, we can tell of the first rays of dawn on a third day, the **beginning of a New Creation; of the morning stars singing as at the** first over death's final defeat; and of a risen Lord, seated at the right hand of Power, and yet mysteriously, wondrously, ever present in his Spirit in every congregation gathered together in his name.

There in the midst of that gathered people, we can point to God's working still: a church sustained through no merit or instrumentality of its own; a man forgiven of all his guilty past; a woman enabled to carry a burden of constant pain in serenity; a couple empowered to sustain a marriage against the onslaughts of hell; a child guided; a future promised; hope made certain and sure; and everywhere, always, a love wound round us that will not let us go, so that our mood in the midst of our clinging sin can yet be one of joy; and singing—in every corner of the world, God's people singing—because "the kingdom of this world is become the Kingdom of our Lord and of his Christ. Hallelujah!"[3]

We preachers need to labor over our words, so that they may mirror at least a hint of such a God of glory, though we know that heaven and the highest heaven cannot contain him, much less our awkward phrases. But God has chosen us to interpret for our people the wonders of his ways in his universe; to point out in every home and town the traces of his footsteps; to cause our people to remember all his faithful working, and to wind their hearts about his promise of his working still. It is little wonder we echo the awe of Luther—"Although I am old and experienced in speaking, I tremble whenever I ascend the pulpit." We preachers are called to be nothing less than the mediators of the speaking and doing of God.

BY WHAT AUTHORITY?

We need to be very clear about the nature and limits of our authority, however. Too many of us, enraptured by the high nature of our calling, have exchanged the glory of God for the glorification of "me" and have ended up preaching ourselves, relying on our own thoughts, our own technical skills to manipulate our people into placing their trust in a gospel according to nothing but us and our opinions.

The one basis of our authority is the Holy Scriptures, and if we do not preach out of them, we should not be preaching at all. We have to do with God in the Christian ministry; all else is of secondary concern. We are dealing with his relationship with us and the consequences of that relationship for human life in the world. Ours alone among all professions makes the unique confession that persons and universe cannot be understood fully except in their relationship with God. Affairs of the pulpit and church are God-centered, or else they are of the devil.

The living God has made himself known to us through the history and confessions, the letters and prayers, the songs and sagas—the varied literary genres that make up the Bible. There, through a history that spans more than two thousand years, God has chosen to reveal himself—first through a unique folk called Israel and then fully in Israel's offspring, Jesus Christ, "the son of David, the son of Abraham." But that revelation is not a communication of static and dead-letter information, as if the manifestation of the living God could be encapsuled in ideas about him. No, the revelation of God given to us through the Holy Scriptures is a "working"—an effective act by which we are forgiven and brought back into relation with our Creator and set into the wilderness of "the glorious liberty of the children of God," to begin a journey of obedience toward a promised place of fulfillment, where death has no hold on us and evil is done away once and for all. In short, the biblical story becomes our story through our recall of it and is recapitulated in our experience. As God worked in and through Israel and Jesus Christ, so he uses the story of them to work the same way in our lives. What Israel was—the people accompanied by God—the Christian Church becomes, through the story. What Jesus Christ did—reconcile the world to God—his story continues to do for us, and indeed for all generations of Christians who will ever come after.

It is because the biblical story functions in this unique manner that the church has designated the Bible as "canon" and has given it a place above all other authorities as the one measure of faith and practice. The Bible was not arbitrarily chosen by the early church as some fixed and eternal rule. The Bible became the authority for the church because the church learned, over decades of worship and practice, that the biblical story was the one story that created and sustained its life. Through no other story did groups of sinners find themselves transformed into forgiven communities and empowered to live new and godly lives. Through no other story did God and his Son draw so near in the Spirit to those little communities of faith and guide and overshadow their daily existence. Through no other story was the church given such unassailable hope and the assurance of eternal life. Through no other story was the life lived by Jesus Christ made a possibility for imitation by his followers.

So it is still today for us. The vision of human life embodied in the ways and words, in the death and resurrection of Jesus Christ, becomes enfleshed in our daily existence only by the power of the God who works with us through the words of the Holy Scripture. If we want to live Christian lives, there is no source of empowerment other than the story of Jesus Christ, with which finally the whole Bible is concerned. Through its story God works to change us into the image of his Son by the action of the Spirit. No other teaching, no other history, no other mystery known to humankind can make that claim or exhibit the unique and universal people God has created through the sacred history. It is because of its fruits that we have come to invest the story of the Bible with its unique authority.

To be sure, there is other literature in the church which deals with the working of God: creeds, prayers, hymns, devotional tractates, traditions of the Fathers, even modern theologies and commentaries and personal testimonies. And these all can serve as guides to the preacher, continuing the testimony to what God is doing in the midst of his people and offering the assurance that faith's Subject is real and faithful to his promises. Some communions, such as the Christian Scientists and the Latter-day Saints, have even elevated some later testimonies to an equal place alongside the Scriptures. But the truth is that all these later witnesses stand or fall by their faithfulness to the biblical revelation, and we continually discard or change or reformulate such testimonies in the church, because we find them to be inadequate or partial or too time-bound in their mediation of the living God. They are valuable witnesses to the ongoing work of God in human life, but they are incapable of creating and sustaining the life of the church across all the centuries, as the biblical story has done.

In the same manner, there are modern movements and literature, both religious and secular, which our generation has sometimes found very helpful: poetry, drama, transcendental meditation, transactional analysis, religious cults of every kind. Their devotees will swear to their ability to lead them into more wholistic or more transcendentally aware ways of living. We need not dispute such claims. We need only ask if that which is being effected by such literature and cults is a new relationship with the God and Father of our Lord Jesus Christ as he is known in his fullness through the biblical story. It is out of that relationship that the new life of eternal and abundant living in the New Age issues. Once again the Scriptures are the measuring canon, and indeed, by placing all things under their authority, we prevent that pursuit after the latest fad—that experience of being "blown about by every wind of doctrine," of which the apostle Paul has warned us.

Clearly, if we preachers are to be the mediators to our people of the speaking and doing of the true God, we must be the interpreters of the one story through which that God has revealed himself—the story of the Bible. Through our speaking, that story must become our people's story, for in it they are judged and redeemed and made citizens of that kingdom of God which has become reality in Jesus Christ.

Creativity in the pulpit, therefore, has to do with creativity *in relation to the biblical story*. The means we choose to awaken the ears and touch the hearts and open the lives of our congregations to God's re-creation of them must not distort the nature and course of the biblical story. For example, if our preaching promises our people a new life in God, but without the death of their old lives—if we preach only Easter's forgiveness, but not Good Friday's judgment—we have drastically altered the course of that biblical history out of which Christian personality and community are born.

Further still, if in enthusiasm for our own cleverness, we leave the biblical story behind altogether, we will have forfeited all possibility of new Christian life for our people. And it is perhaps that forfeiture which marks so much of what passes for creativity in the pulpit today. For example, a dialogue sermon that does nothing more than discuss a current topic, with no reference to the will and working of the biblical God, may provide an interesting conversation piece for the congregation and prompt their ongoing reflection. But it is not properly to be called a sermon, for a sermon has to do with the immediate action of God. And unless it is followed by the biblical Word, it will transform no lives—at least not in the way God in Christ transforms them. That action of God through the medium of human words is what preaching is all about. And the imaginative presentation of that action defines and constitutes creative preaching.

① Biblical preaching is the power to transform lives.

② imaginative preaching.

II. THE NATURE AND DEVELOPMENT OF CREATIVITY

A preacher's tools are words, shaped into the rhythms and cadences, the fortissimos and whispers, the conversation and confrontation of oral speech. To neglect the mastery of words is to be like a carpenter who throws away his saw and sets out to fashion a piece of fine furniture, using nothing but an ax. We may hack away at a congregation with tools totally inappropriate to their purpose—dull words, misleading sentences, repetitious paragraphs, ineffective illustrations. Or we may take up the fine tool of language, honed and polished to a cutting edge, and then trust that God will use it to fashion his people—his "work of art in Christ" (Eph. 2:10). The committed preachers—the faithful servants of God—do not neglect their tools!

WHAT LANGUAGE DOES

To understand the importance of mastering words, however, we must ask what they do. So often we conceive of speech as simply the conveyance of information. We set forth our ideas in words, or we ask others for theirs. And preaching understood in such a framework has little more than a cognitive function—the communication of the ideas of the preacher to the minds of the congregation, to be accepted or rejected, depending upon the persuasiveness and authority of the argument.

But language is much more than simply the bearer of ideas. *LANGUAGE* Language brings reality into being for a person and orders and shapes the person's universe. There is a profound story in Genesis, in which the Lord God brings the beasts and the birds which he has created to Adam for naming, and "whatever the man called every living creature, that was its name" (2:19-20). By this act of naming, Adam gives existence and order to the creatures around him. Now they are "there" for Adam; they can be referred to apart from himself; his act of speech organizes and gives reality to the setting in which he lives. We sometimes wonder why biologists and zoologists go to the trouble of making long lists of every class and species of living creature and organism, but they are doing exactly what Adam did: They are positing and ordering their reality. Language actually makes our universe exist for us and sets us off from it as also having reality.

In her autobiography, Helen Keller tells what it meant to her when she could finally identify water by a word.

> Suddenly I felt a misty consciousness as of something forgotten—a thrill of returning thought; and somehow the mystery of language was revealed to me. I knew then that "w-a-t-e-r" meant the wonderful cool something that was flowing over my hand. That living word awakened my soul, gave it light, hope, joy, set it free! There were barriers still, it is true, but barriers that could in time be swept away.
>
> Thus I came up out of Egypt and stood before Sinai, and a power divine touched my spirit and gave it sight, so that I beheld many wonders. And from the sacred mountain I heard a voice which said, "Knowledge is love and light and vision."[1]

The world was not "there" for Helen Keller until she could use words to speak it, and she says she knew no sorrow, no love, no joy until she could order her reality in language. "In the beginning was the Word . . . All things were made through him, and without him was not anything made that was made" (John 1:1, 3). There was nothing until God spoke the Word. And for us too, there is the void, the chaos—the primeval *tohu wabbohu*, devoid of reality—until we speak the words. Human words, like God's Word, bring our universe into being and order, and perhaps the fact that we can speak and so create a world is the residual evidence that we were made in the image of God.

Put another way, human beings live by the images of reality created by their words. As essayist Joan Didion has said, "We tell ourselves stories in order to live."[2] The story of our nation or of our family becomes our identification—our means of knowing who we are. The recounting of a tragedy or of a death becomes the way we order such life-threatening events and gain mastery over them. Neighborhood gossip or rumor is used to establish our secure place in the pecking order of society; we impose an order on it and place ourselves at the top. "We live entirely," says Didion, "by the imposition of a narrative line upon disparate images, by the 'ideas' with which we have learned to freeze the shifting phantasmagoria which is our actual experience." There in the images and myths and imaginations of the heart, all created by our words, we order and shape and maintain the structures of our personal and corporate worlds.

It follows, therefore, that if we want to change someone's life from non-Christian to Christian; from dying to living; from despairing to hoping; from anxious to certain; from corrupted to whole, we must change the images—the imaginations of the heart—in short, the words by which that person lives.

There is no guarantee at all that the reality a person has constructed for him- or herself corresponds to the objective nature of the universe. Advertisers and politicians have long known that if something is said often enough; if suggestive words are constantly repeated, people will come to accept the suggestion as the truth—that is, the words will become the shapers of their reality. Thus Hitler's propaganda, dinned into the ears of the German public day after day, led that people finally to believe that they were a master race and that they had a perfect right to decide who should live or die. The words; the Big Lie; the corrupted language—these became the creators of German reality, just as Churchill's mobilization of the English language on his tiny isle became the life-giving force which sustained the British reality of no defeat, ever.

Sometimes a person's reality can be changed by changing the connotations of his words. For example, the word "black" has long been associated in Western culture with evil, darkness, death. The villains wear the black hats in our Western movies. The poet writes of his suffering in terms of darkness:

> Out of the night that covers me,
>   Black as the Pit from pole to pole,
> I thank whatever gods may be
>   For my unconquerable soul.[3]

Much of this usage may have stemmed from the fact that writers of the Bible used darkness and night as the symbols of final evil. To quote only one of many passages: "And the city has no need of sun or moon to shine upon it, for the glory of God is its light, and its lamp is the Lamb . . . and its gates shall never be shut by day—and there shall be no night there" (Rev. 21:23, 25).

For a people created with black skins, however, such images of darkness prove devastating, and the connotations of the word "black" must be totally altered, or a black people can have no pride in itself and no sense of worth and goodness. Its slogan therefore becomes "black is beautiful," and by that new combination of words, a new reality is slowly created.

The inner imaginations of the heart are changed when a person's language is changed, and the images by which that person lives are altered into a new experience of reality. And everywhere the Bible insists that new life involves this change of heart—this inner transformation of personality by the working of the Word. Thus it is that Yahweh writes new Words on the hearts of his sinful people. According to Jeremiah, Judah's sin had been engraved on the tablet of her heart with a "pen of iron," a "point of diamond" (17:1). But in the New Age, under the new covenant, Yahweh's words are written there, instead (31:31-34). "These words which I command you this day shall be upon your heart," Israel is told in the central commandment of Deuteronomy. "The Lord our God is one Lord; and you shall love the Lord your God with all your heart, and with all your soul, and with all your might" (6:6). Such are to be the Words that create and shape all reality for the people of God.

So it is too for the Christian. God has spoken a final Word in Jesus Christ, summing up and fulfilling all his Words that have gone before and indicating the meaning and purpose of all that is to come after. And that Word—that speech of God's—is to be the bearer of reality for his children—the image and sign and interpreter of what God is truly like and of what we and our society and our world are truly to become. The Word of God in his incarnate Son mediates truth (cf. John 1) and bears with it true connotation and the true shape of human existence. God's Word in Jesus Christ is the objective nature of reality, to which all our realities are to conform. Christ's relationships with human beings are to be our relationships. His unbroken fellowship with his Father is to be our fellowship. His vision of God in control of all nature and history, destiny, and fate, is to be our vision. His universal kingdom is to be the realm—the reality—in which we live.

Obviously, however, the existences we create for ourselves differ radically from the reality spoken by God in his Word.

> Woe to those who call evil good
>   and good evil,
> who put darkness for light
>   and light for darkness,
> who put bitter for sweet
>   and sweet for bitter!
> —Isaiah 5:20

Our language becomes corrupted language, in which we exchange God's good reality for our evil ways. All the imaginations of the thoughts of our hearts—the images by which we live—become centered round self and pride and gain, until they are "only evil continually," and the good and just and peaceful world intended by the Word of God in his creation is replaced by the reality created by our corrupted hearts.

They bend their tongue like a bow;
    falsehood and not truth has grown strong in the land;
for they proceed from evil to evil,
    and they do not know me, says the Lord.
                                                        —Jeremiah 9:3

Rhetorician Richard M. Weaver has even maintained that our moral confusion in modern America is partly due to our failure to insist upon no compromise in definition.[4] Put another way, it is certainly due to the fact that we do not conform our hearts to God's; that his thoughts are not our thoughts and his ways not our ways, because we refuse to accept his Word as the definition of our reality. It is to be not we who live, but Christ who liveth in us; not our minds, but the mind of Christ; not our words, but God's Word which creates and defines our thought and action. God's Word in Jesus Christ, the One in whom we live and move and have our being, is to be the creator and shaper of our world, because in him is the true definition of life. Apart from him there is only chaos and darkness and death. "In him was life, and the life was the light of men" (John 1:4). We preachers are called by our God to proclaim his life-giving Word; to use human words in such a fashion that they grasp our people's hearts with the truth of Christ. The images and pictures, the desires and visions, the motivations and dreams by which we and our people live are to be shaped by the Word of God, until the reality that is Christ's is our reality, and our lives are conformed to his image. We cannot fulfill that calling, however, simply by repeating the words of the Bible, because for many, the images those words bear and the connotations they carry have themselves become corrupted. For many in modern society, the word "God" now signals nothing more than a meaningless blur—a great Someone in the great somewhere who accepts us into relation with himself, no matter what we do. "Sin," for the average congregation, usually immediately carries the meaning "sex." "Love" may be an emotional feeling, "bigger than both of us," which can be as ephemeral as a cloud or, paradoxically, destructive of an earlier marriage covenant. We have the task therefore of preaching the gospel in words that do not distort its meaning, and this often involves the use of language quite different from that of the Bible.

In the same vein, there are those for whom the biblical words have lost their power—their ability to change the images and reality by which those people live. The biblical language has been accepted by them as a static "given." They assume that they know what it means and that they need nothing but perhaps an additional item of information or an occasional reminder to remember what they already know. Such persons may indeed be enthusiastic about the biblical language. They may insist that their preacher mouth exactly the words they expect. They may zealously defend some English translation of the Bible. They may maintain that no one is a Christian who does not accept the objective truth of one or another biblical sentence. But when it comes to actually shaping the way they live their lives, the biblical language and the images it carries have lost all power to influence. The words have become dead letter and not living symbols of reality; they have been separated from the imaginations of the thoughts of the heart. As Isaiah puts it,

> Because this people draw near with their mouth
> and honor me with their lips,
> while their hearts are far from me,
> and their fear of me is a commandment of men learned by rote;
> therefore, behold, I will again do marvelous things with
> this people.
>
> —Isaiah 29:13-14

That is, God will act in judgment.

Ezekiel describes the separation of words and heart in the figure of a heart turned to stone; those with stony hearts can only be saved by God's gift of hearts of flesh (36:26). Words must have the power to get at our inner imaginations, and often the preacher must use new words to present the biblical message. Otherwise it remains a lifeless literature for many familiar with it.

We cannot preach, therefore, by simply repeating what "the Bible says." Evangelist Billy Graham has gone about the world with that phrase. In an article in *Christianity Today*, he explained his rationale. "I stopped trying to prove that the Bible was true. I had settled in my own mind that it was, and this faith was conveyed to the audience. Over and over again I found myself saying 'The Bible says.' "[5] But the question is, What perception of reality is conveyed by the words of the Bible? What is the congregation seeing and hearing and thinking and experiencing when it hears what the Bible says? And does that perception have any power to influence or to change their lives? More important still, Is the biblical message truly conveyed by framing it in propositions and principles and truths, or is that hermeneutical method itself a distortion of the biblical message? We shall discuss that question at length in the next chapter.

Graham has seemingly had success with his evangelistic campaigns, and his method may have conveyed to some the reality intended by the biblical writers. But there is no doubt that the response of many persons in our society to the words of the Bible is a complete misunderstanding or distortion of the biblical intentions, and we preachers have often done nothing more than confirm our people in their secular life-styles. The Word has fallen on rocky ground and has never borne fruit, to use Mark's figure. Or to refer again to Ezekiel's usage: The stony hearts have never been transformed into hearts of flesh, with which to love God and obey his will and walk in his ways.

Between the Word of the Bible and the ways of our people in the world, God has chosen to set the persons of us, his preachers. Our task therefore is one of so framing the Word in the words of our sermons that Jesus Christ fills the imaginations of the hearts of our people and becomes the image—the sole reality—by which they conduct their lives.

> I had heard of thee by the hearing of the ear,
>   but now my eye sees thee.
>   —Job 42:5

To prompt that confession on the part of our people is the purpose of our preaching—by the imaginative power of our words, to enable our people to see—to see God in Jesus Christ and to know that hearty fellowship with him in the Spirit, which leads to life and good and the reality of his abundant kingdom.

CAN CREATIVITY BE LEARNED?

The question which immediately arises, of course, is whether we can learn to be preachers who can so shape language that it gets at people's hearts and changes their entire perceptions of reality and the way they lead their lives. When faced with such a task, we are often likely to demur in the words of Moses, "Oh, my Lord, I am not eloquent, either heretofore or since thou hast spoken to thy servant; but I am slow of speech and of tongue. . . . Oh, my Lord, send, I pray, some other person" (Exod. 4:10, 13). But if Moses and the myriad witnesses after him had not accepted the task, you and I would not now be Christians. The Christian gospel has spread through the world because it is possible to communicate it; because it is possible to make creative preachers out of people like fisherman Peter and tentmaker Paul and tens of thousands of other ordinary folk with the talents of you and me.

We do have to work at the task, however. God is not going to do for us the work he has called us to perform. And as with all the jobs God gives human beings to do, there is a discipline to be undergone—a purifying, a tempering in the fires of struggle and devotion—before we are fit instruments to be used in his service. "Discipline" and "disciple" are formed from the same root. There is no way to be the latter without undergoing the former.

The very first step in the discipline of learning to be a preacher is that of mastering basic English usage. American schools are now turning out, year after year, hundreds of thousands of students who cannot write a proper English sentence, much less a well-formed paragraph, and these illiterates are showing up in our pulpits. Thus our congregations are hearing phrases such as "between he and I," "there are less Christians today," "O Lord, we would ask that you bless us," "his robe was divided between the four soldiers," "every one of us are," "I wouldn't hardly believe," "let me pursue this subject farther," "hopefully things will get better"—the list of grammatical errors could be extended almost indefinitely. Piled on top of these in pulpit speech are misplaced modifiers, participial phrases attached to the wrong subject, nouns used as verbs, adverbs turned into adjectives, split infinitives, words misused or mispronounced, garbled sentences, wandering paragraphs, confusing transitional phrases—in short, fog, pulpit fog, through which our people try desperately to see some light of meaning.

Preachers often try to excuse their torture of the English language by saying, "My people know me. I talk like they do. They know what I mean." But in the service of the gospel of God, such carelessness will not do. We may think our people know what we mean, but we must not leave it to chance. Every sentence, every paragraph must be absolutely clear. "It has pleased God through the folly of the message we preach to save those who believe." The eternal life or death of our people may depend on their knowing what we mean. If a person is dying, a respirator with holes in its tank will not start him breathing again. An approximation of the word of the cross will not often lead to a resurrection.

If you did not learn proper English usage in school, then learn it on your own. Work your way through an English grammar, study *The Elements of Style*, by Strunk and White, or read Edwin Newman's popular book, *Strictly Speaking*.[6] Then practice writing sentences and paragraphs, critique the grammar in your letters, become conscious of how you express yourself in conversation. Those who know how to write well are very often those who express themselves well in a sermon. Practice writing! Practice! Practice! until you have mastered your basic language tool.

After that, begin to hone and polish the tool. English is one of the most beautiful and powerful languages in the world. In its range of vocabulary and nuance and phrase; in its flexibility of expression; in the cadences of its rhythms and the sounds of its vowels, it has few linguistic equals. Listen (I use that verb purposely) to what a master writer can do with the English language.

It is easy enough to say . . . that when the last ding-dong of doom has clanged and faded from the last worthless rock hanging tideless in the last red and dying evening that even then there will still be one more sound; that of his [man's] puny inexhaustible voice still talking. I refuse to accept this. I believe that man will not merely endure: he will prevail.[7]

In that brief excerpt are imagery, onomatopoeia, variety in pace, meaning, conviction. The passage appeals to eye, ear, mind, heart—the total person. The English language can be used to capture a congregation for God. Indeed, if our speech is expanded to the limits of the capacity of our language, there are few more powerful instruments for motivating and moving human beings. Preaching has died, not because oral speech is ineffective—it has suffered fatal wounds only when the preachers have not mastered speaking.

Words are the preacher's instrument and the study of language an inexpendable pursuit. Such study should be carried on in a systematic and never-ending fashion. First, the preacher should constantly practice the art of observation and imaginative description. How would you describe, for example, the child playing in the yard on your block, or the reactions of that child when her father comes home from the office? What words would you use to portray the people in the airport lounge, or at the grocery store checkout counter, or in the Sunday school classroom? How would you picture your garden flowers, or your neighbor, or your reaction to them? Practice putting the incidents and scenes of everyday into words; see if you can make them come alive in a few brief and vivid words. It is an exercise one can carry on while waiting for a green light, or while getting dressed, or while walking the distance from parsonage to church; it aids the imagination in mentally trying out and turning over words until expressions are found that will enable our listeners to see what we have seen.

Second, the preacher should listen carefully to the words of others. I have a poet friend who always goes to public meetings or lectures with a small notebook in her purse. When she hears a memorable phrase, an imaginative description, a vivid metaphor, she writes it down, not only for the purpose of using that phrase or word in her writing, but mainly, to stretch the limits of her imagination and observation.

We can and do sometimes borrow the phrases of others in our preaching, of course. T. S. Eliot's capsule summary of the meaninglessness of suburbia: "We have measured out our lives in coffee spoons"; Thornton Wilder's portrayal of the loss of family relations: "We never have time to look at one another"; Christopher Fry's recognition of the cosmic drama at stake in human life: "Affairs are now soul size"—such masterful portrayals are too good to ignore. But primarily, the preacher should listen to others' words in order to improve his own, and the major source for such improvement is in literature. Constant reading helps us find the words to engage the hearts and minds and wills of our congregations.

When you find telling phrases and expressions in the material you read, write them down, store them up, study them. Preachers, unfortunately, often read simply to find sermon illustrations; far too few read with the purpose of expanding and improving their use of the English language. We learn to write well by reading well; we learn to speak well by "listening" to great language from the pens of our best novelists, dramatists, poets, historians, essayists, biographers, preachers. As Winston Churchill said of his schooling, we get the feel of an English sentence under our belts. Pleasing rhythms, pictorial vocabulary, felicity of phrase, the proper order of words in emphasis—these become second nature to the preacher who is constantly absorbing their use in great literature.

Preachers should read constantly, not only to master language, but because we also have the second task of growing as human beings. If we read only to find illustrations, we have never let ourselves be engaged by the written word. And how limited and ingrown remain our thoughts and perceptions of the world! In literature—all types of literature—are distilled the history, the thoughts, the feelings of the human race. Our worlds and our minds and characters are expanded by sharing that distillation. Who of us has ever experienced before what we experience through Tolkien's writings, or Melville's, or, lately, Annie Dillard's or Lewis Thomas'? In great literature is the nourishment for the expansion of our lives.

Third, preachers should read constantly in order to know our world. We have the task of speaking the images of the gospel to a society already living on particular images. Behind the words, the expressions, the slogans and jargons of our time are the mental perceptions, myths, and imaginations that are shaping our people's lives—world-views, self-views, views of society and nature and God which are determining what our people do and believe and plan and dream. If we intend to talk of God to our society, we need to know who they already think God is. If we are to speak of guilt and forgiveness, of injustice and justification, we need to know how our people already perceive themselves. For example, do they believe themselves generous masters over wrong, or helpless pawns of evil fate? Knowing these beliefs can make all the difference in how and what is preached, and it is from the literature of our time that a preacher can gain such knowledge. Newspapers, magazines, current drama and poetry and books—these mirror our society, as do TV programs, movies, art, ads, dances, fads, and happenings. The preacher must be a constant student of the age reflected in the media around him, or else he may, in his speaking, make no contact with the actual people sitting in the pews before him.

Further, the preacher should read, go to plays and movies, and study art and poetry and various media expressions, in order to learn from them the fine art of communication. For example, no comedian or actor in this country has ever succeeded without an exquisite sense of timing—the exact knowledge of when to pause and when to speak; of when to talk rapidly and when to slow down. Every preacher could profit from listening and absorbing the sense of timing that is exhibited continually on America's stages.

Again, no great artists, be they singers or actresses or poets, ever present their art apart from a certain restraint—a control, a sense of appropriateness, even an understatement—giving the impression that there are depths of power and expression that remain still untapped. Artists do not shout at us, nor do they engage in unbridled emotion—a truth most contemporary rock entertainers have, incidentally, never absorbed. The preacher can profit from imitating that emotional and oral restraint. I often need to remind homiletics students that they cannot attempt to grip a congregation with excitement throughout an entire twenty-minute sermon. The restraint of the artist respects the integrity and privacy of the listener and gives the personality of the hearer space in which to feel and think and respond and thus to move into a new reality.

Finally, artists, of whatever medium, rarely confront us directly with the demand that we accept their words or adopt their views and perceptions. The poet does not say, "This is truth; believe it." The dramatist does not insist, "This is the only way human life is." The painter does not imply, "This is the one shape of reality." Instead, these artists present to us that which they see, in words so evocative and expressions so suggestive that we are enabled to enter into their experiences and to see the world as they see it. They prompt us, by their imagery, their imagination, their nuance of expression, to live through what they have lived and to know what they have known. Thus they enlarge our vision and give us new possibilities for seeing and doing.

Insofar as it shares these methods of communication, preaching, too, is artistry—the practice of fine art. But it is never art for art's sake; its goal is the communication of the gospel. It is never manipulative; the preacher is not attempting to move a congregation against its will or to control its free response. It is never selfish; the preacher is not trying to persuade the congregation to adopt his or her own private and subjective views of reality. Rather, the preacher is one who has shared in the communion of saints; who has become a member of that people with whom, through the ages, the eternal God has seen fit to dwell. "Is it not in thy going with us . . . that we are distinct, I and thy people, from all other people that are upon the face of the earth?" (Exod. 33:16). The preacher is one who has joined company with those who have seen "the light of the knowledge of the glory of God in the face of Christ"; who has believed and so now speaks (II Cor. 4:6, 13). The preacher is one who has known, intimately, new life in Christ in the new reality of the kingdom of God and who now, by imagery and imagination and evocation of experiences, attempts to enable the congregation to know it too.

> That which was from the beginning, which we have heard, which we have seen with our eyes, which we have looked upon and touched with our hands . . . that which we have seen and heard we proclaim also to you, so that you may have fellowship with us; and our fellowship is with the Father and with his Son Jesus Christ.
>
> —I John 1:1, 3

The preacher/artist helps enable the congregation to live into that from which he lives—the company of God and Christ and the Holy Spirit and the faithful of all times and places.

CHRISTIAN DISCIPLINE

We come now to that final discipline of the preacher/disciple, without which all else is futile: the discipline of study and life in community and prayer and obedience—in short, the discipline of Christian faith and practice. Contrary to popular belief, we are not free human beings. As Paul would express it, we are either slaves to sin or slaves of Jesus Christ. And only Christ sets us free from the bondage of our dying selves and corrupted world, to be the persons in community that God intended us to be. We enter into the freedom of the Christian person by taking Christ's yoke upon us and learning of him. We become the creatures we were meant to be by becoming Jesus Christ's.

Let me emphasize that it is not an overnight process. A sudden conversion experience may, for some, change the direction and motivation of their lives. Saul of Tarsus had the course of his life turned around on the road to Damascus. But afterward, he assured us that he was continuing to run a race for which he constantly disciplined himself, "lest after preaching to others I myself should be disqualified" (I Cor. 9:24-27). He had not already attained his final goal; he was not already perfect; "but I press on to make it my own, because Christ Jesus has made me his own. . . . Let those of us who are mature be thus minded" (Phil. 2:12, 15). Living the Christian life is a constant race—a continual discipline, involving the decisions we make every day, the influences we let rule our hearts, a steady saying of yes, in every situation, to the yoke of Jesus Christ.

If we do not practice that discipline and rehearse that yes, how can we know that God whom we want our people to know? How can we enable them to see, if we have never seen? How can we help them follow Christ if we do not follow him and are not absolutely certain he is with us always? When once asked the basis of Charles Spurgeon's success as a preacher, his brother replied, "I think it lies in the fact that he loves Jesus of Nazareth and Jesus of Nazareth loves him."[8] Or as Augustine put it, "What I live by, I impart."

A clergy friend of mine, a victim of terminal cancer and thus forced to give up his pulpit, wrote shortly before his death, "You ask for my insights on preaching. I guess the one thing that I see as I look over a ministry from which I am now at some distance removed is the importance of preaching what one has experienced. Otherwise, it's hearsay."

The gospel cannot be lived out by one who has it only as secondhand information, nor can it be communicated by the preacher who has inherited it simply by hearsay—little snippets gathered here and there from the latest books and conversations; unexamined propositions garnered by growing up in a church or in a pious family; thoughts borrowed from one's fellow preachers and the commentators and theologians, from the professors one had in seminary or, worst of all, from canned sermon outlines and books of illustrations. Such secondhand experiences of the gospel result in scissors-and-paste sermons—ideas developed around the thoughts of others and strung together in an outline. They may make logical sense, but they will seldom reveal the living God, because the preacher who speaks them has no sense of that God and communicates no experience of having lived in him and loved him.

Our people want credible witnesses. There is the rumor abroad in our land that the Christian life is impossible to live and that the sacred story is a fairy tale, comforting for our elder citizens and good ethical guidance for children, but having little relevance to the hard realities of life in consumer America. It is science and technology which reveal and handle the shape of reality in the twentieth century; the church is useful simply to keep some moral pressure on us, to pray in our stead to any gods that be, and to ease our passage ritually through some of the more significant changes and crises of life—such is the general view of many in the American marketplace. But if you set in the midst of all that a preacher who truly knows God, who loves him with a burning love, and who woos a congregation into sharing such knowledge and passion, the hungry come—the desperate hungry sheep to the shepherd who feeds them. "Sir, we wish to see Jesus" (John 12:21). That request of Philip is still the deep longing of our people's hearts, and it is the requirement laid upon our preaching and upon our lives.

How do we know God for ourselves? We know him through deep and sustained and continual study of the Bible, and we shall have much more to say on that subject in the next chapter. But right now, that statement implies that in the ministry, it is not sufficient to study the Bible only when we have a sermon to write, or a Sunday school class to lead, or a Bible study to conduct. It is not sufficient even to read a passage of the Bible every day in our personal or family devotions. We are to know God's Word through and through. It is the bread by which we live and with which we feed our people. It is the background commentary on every experience we have and every decision we make. It is our understanding of ourselves and of our fellows and of our world, because it mediates to us what God is doing in all of these, and where we stand and what we are in relation to his activity. There, through that sacred story, God becomes real Presence—or perhaps better, central Actor in our every day.

It takes work to know God through the Bible that way—hard, concentrated, sustained study and learning—care with the text and scholarly probing of its layers; imaginative re-creation of its history and milieu; reflection on its nuances of theology and traditions, until the thrust of each pericope stands forth fully and the Voice is heard and the Actor seen, and the dead written words become for us the Word of our living King. Every minister, every day, should set aside time for *work* with the Word, or he will not know the God he has been called to make known to his congregation.

There is a strange dialogue which starts haltingly and then becomes constant, when one studies the Bible—a dialogue between that Word and the life one is living. We begin to see things we never saw before: the fact that there are no natural laws, but only the faithfulness of creation's Sustainer—as G. K. Chesterton once commented in poetic fashion, "The sun doesn't rise by natural law; it rises because God says, 'Get up and do it again' "; the realization that

> There lives the dearest freshness deep down things;
> And though the last lights off the black West went
> Oh, morning, at the brown brink eastward, springs—
> Because the Holy Ghost over the bent
> World broods with warm breast and with ah! bright wings.[9]

Even a common field of wild flowers becomes a triumphant reminder—"Not even Solomon in all his glory . . ."

We begin to trust more fully. Our own life is not self-contained and dependent on personal success for its meaning, but rather planned, guided, woven together with other lives of loved ones in a providence that is moving us all toward a final goal. We find ourselves having no need to justify our own importance, no need to answer back when attacked, no need to rail against life's disappointments and tragedies. We are beset behind and before by One who knows us altogether (cf. Ps. 139). That which seems evil on the face of it turns out to be meant by God for good (cf. Gen. 50:20). We are afflicted at times but never crushed; perplexed but never despairing; struck down but not destroyed (cf. II Cor. 4:8-9), because we find that the words of Christ's promises are really true: He does not leave us desolate; he comes to us (John 14:18), and we are borne, carried (cf. Isa. 46:3-4), even when we are wrong and have failed miserably to love or to do the right thing, because we are forgiven, justified, accepted wholly by the mercy of Christ, quite apart from all deserving and all consequences of our own stupid or sinful actions. In short, the preacher who knows the Bible through and through daily tests that knowledge in his or her own living, and that which has been read becomes that which is experienced. As Rudolph Bohren once wrote, "My sole title as a preacher of the Gospel to proclaim the delivering Word lies in the fact that it has indeed delivered, and daily goes on delivering, my own eyes from tears, my feet from falling, my soul from death."[10] The Word of Christ proves trustworthy.

The more we live out of the biblical Word, the more we also find ourselves implanted in a community of the faithful. There is nothing else like the fellowship of those who singly and together depend on Christ for their guidance and forgiveness and personal goodness. A lack of self-seeking, an integrity of action upon which we can depend, a spirit of mutual helpfulness pervades such a community; and always just below the surface, there is rollicking humor and laughter, because these are people who know that their times and lives are in God's good hands. The amazing thing, moreover, is that such persons are to be found in almost every Christian congregation. We can go anywhere on the face of the earth and yet find a unifying bond with fellow Christians, because life in the Word necessarily issues in such community. Part of the discipline of daily dialogue with the Word therefore involves practicing this Christian fellowship— opening ourselves to it, searching out those in the congregation who know what it is to live in Christ, letting their faith instruct us, and consciously subordinating our own will to "the Spirit of unity in the bond of peace." Sometimes the faith of such small groups of Christians can carry the preacher through times of doubt and discouragement. Always their existence is testimony to the working of God in his church. As Reinhold Niebuhr once wrote of his Detroit congregation: "The people are a little discouraged. Some of them seem to doubt whether the church will survive. But there are a few who are the salt of the earth, and if I make a go of this they will be more responsible than they will ever know." And, again, of a faithful elderly woman within that congregation: "She thanks me for praying with her and imagines that I am doing her a favor to come to see her. But I really come for selfish reasons—because I leave that home with a more radiant faith of my own. My confidence in both man and God is strengthened."[11] In Christian fellowship, we experience the action of the Word of God, and in that dialogue our lives are shaped and sustained, so that we may confidently say from the pulpit, "I know whom I have believed" (II Tim. 1:12).

Part of the participation in Christian fellowship, of course, is participation in the community's worship, and that too is a necessary part of Christian discipline. One sometimes meets seminary professors who rarely go to church on Sunday. More common is the preacher who leads the worship of his or her own congregation, but really is not engaged in it. Instead, the preacher's mind is on the details of the service, the size of the congregation, the impression he or she is making, or the sermon to come. As W. E. Sangster has remarked, "They stand and hand it out to the people. 'Here is a hymn for you to sing. When you've done that, I'll give you something more.' "[12] Such a stance is a denial of the very Word the preacher is called to preach: the fact that we are one in Christ; the proclamation that we are never self-sufficient; the truth that our proper attitude before our God is one of praise and self-surrender. We preachers never stand with God over against our people. It is the people and we, one in Christ, assembled before our Sovereign, to sing his praise and to confess our sin and to receive his life-giving action, together. Life in Christ, apart from his body the church, is a mockery of the Word we preach. The Word's action results in the creation of a new community.

Discipline under the Word and daily dialogue with it also involve the continual straining after obedience. When we know the Bible through and through, the outlines of how we are to live in society become rather clear. There are a unique ethos and ethic to the Christian life which set it off from other manners of living, and in our world it is not easy to practice that peculiar Way. It involves how we use our money and what we do in our marriages. It dictates our attitudes and actions toward the poor and helpless, toward politics and international affairs. It intrudes into family quarrels and neighborhood responsibilities. It has to do with how we raise our children and with recreation and entertainment. Always, everywhere, the Christian tries to respond to the world with the "mind of Christ," seeking that which is honorable and pure, lovely and gracious and excellent in the sight of God (Phil. 4:8), not in a puritanical legalism but in the freedom with which Christ has set us free (Gal. 5:1). The amazing thing, however, is that the more we live in obedience, the easier we find it to be, the more joy we have in the Word, and the more abundant life becomes. Dialogue with the Word of God, carried out in faithfulness, brings precisely that growth up into the measure of the fullness of Christ and that happiness in him which are promised us by the Word if we are faithful to Christ's commands. "These things I have spoken to you, that my joy may be in you, and that your joy may be full" (John 15:11). That is not an empty assurance, but the reality of what happens to the obedient disciple.

It is not surprising therefore that the final issue of this daily disciplined dialogue with the Word of God is love for him—swelling, passionate, heart-filling love, which takes over our personalities. By living in and through and from the Word of God spoken to us through the Bible, we find ourselves given a new look at the world; forgiven and made alive in our own personalities; enabled to trust; set into a sustaining community; empowered to obey and rejoice. Who can help but love the God who does all that for us? Our fellowship with him becomes "one holy passion, filling all [our] frame," and that in turn results in the life of daily prayer.

I sometimes think we misunderstand the life of prayer: We see it only as a means of seeking God. But we know God primarily through dialogue with the Word, and knowing him thus, we cannot help, then, but pray. Prayer pours out our praise and gratitude for the working of God through his Word; prayer asks that the nourishment of that Word never come to an end, that we continue to be given that "daily bread" from which we have had such joy and guidance; prayer leans on One who has shown himself trustworthy and gracious; prayer asks all things in intercession and petition; prayer is the constant self-surrender of the convinced disciple. In short, prayer is as natural to the preacher who lives from the Word of God as the passionate expression of devotion is to one in love, because living in the Word, we cannot help loving God; and if we love him, we speak with him, pouring out our hearts and souls in the undoubted intimacy of lovers. It has often been noted of pulpit masters that they lead lives of continual and constant prayer. The reason is that they already know the God to whom they pray, and they turn to him as the One from whom they literally live and breathe, seeking even deeper faith, greater knowledge, surer guidance and sustenance. They know that, apart from God, they can do nothing (cf. John 15:4-5).

Word and worship, discipline and devotion, form the circle of the Christian life. We cannot and we should never try to preach the gospel without them.

III. CREATIVE EXEGESIS

One half of the world seems to believe that every poetic symbol with which religion must deal is an exact definition of a concrete or an historical fact; the other half, having learned that this is not the case, can come to no other conclusion but that all religion is based upon fantasy.

Fundamentalists have at least one characteristic in common with most scientists. Neither can understand that poetic and religious imagination has a way of arriving at truth by giving a clue to the total meaning of things without being in any sense an analytic description of detailed facts. The fundamentalists insist that religion is science, and thus they prompt those who know that this is not true to declare that all religious truth is contrary to scientific fact. [1]

—Reinhold Niebuhr

THE NATURE OF THE BIBLICAL WORD

The biblical story is neither fantasy nor science. Rather, it is the confession of faith, across some two thousand years of history, of thousands of witnesses who tell us what God has done in their lives and who call us to share in that experience and in the faithful response to it. The call is issued, however, not in propositional truths about God, for that would appeal only to our intellects, ignoring the biblical happenings and giving us no way to live into them. And the call to faith and obedience is not framed in terms of legalistic demand, for that would leave us without motivating power to respond to what God has done.

No, the biblical story is told in forms which appeal to the

imaginations of our hearts, which call forth the total response of our personalities, and which allow us to enter into its human events as recipients of the divine activity. For example, we are not only told that God is love—that love is defined by a story—of a supper in an upper room and a friend's betrayal; of a prayer and a kiss and a mob in a garden; and of the crow of a cock. Love is pictured through the events of a whipping, a trial, a mocking, and a crown of thorns, and finally by a cross and nails and vinegar and two dying thieves. The love of God is a pictured action in the biblical witness—an action done also to us through the means of the pictures, and therefore an event we experience and to which we can respond.

To use another example, we are not given a carefully shaped dogma about the providence of God, in the Bible. Instead, we are presented with a wisdom novel about the jealousy of brothers, led by hatred to sell their younger brother into slavery and to lie to their father, and about how that human evil nevertheless is used by God to keep his promise to the patriarchs (Gen. 37–50). Or we read the eyewitness narrative of a king who commits adultery and murder, and yet of how God uses those deeds to put an heir whom he loves on the throne of the Davidic empire (II Sam. 6–I Kings 2). In short, in the Bible we see God at work in the actualities of human life, and the hope begins to fill our hearts that perhaps he is at work in the grubby round of our lives also, fulfilling in faithfulness and mercy the promises he has made.

We are not only told that the New Age has dawned in Jesus Christ. Rather, we read stories—all types of stories—of an epileptic son restored whole to his father and of a bent woman enabled to stand up straight; of a prostitute's love accepted and of a rich little subversive's faith rewarded; of a blinding vision on a mountain and of a fish supper in the village of Emmaus. Everywhere along the way, we hear parables and sayings and proverbs, all presented to us once again in pictures, similes, and metaphors, having to do with places of honor at a banquet and with a shepherd looking for a lost sheep; with a son leaving home and returning again; with a traveler being mugged and helped. We not only read the story, we feel it and enter into it; its glad news becomes news *for us,* and its Lord becomes our Lord and Savior.

The Bible does not push a dogma upon us; it lets us enter into events by imagination, until the story becomes our story and we are transformed by it. It often is a source of amazement to us at Christmastime that persons become so kind and thoughtful and that merriment fills the air, in spite of us or our situations. But the reason is that the Christmas season is the one time when the church has learned to go pictorial—when it has forgotten "truths" and "principles" and dead-letter doctrines and settled for wise men and shepherds, kneeling on straw in thousands of creches throughout the breadth of the land. The story is told and pictured and sung, and so it is made our story too, and the angel's announcement is heard by *us* and *we* have a newborn Savior.

Because the story of God's salvation of humankind is presented to us through the heart-stirring genres of the Bible, it therefore follows that if we are to proclaim that story, we should do so in words and forms that will produce the same telling effects. Why turn God's love into a proposition, when in reality it is made up of two thousand years of actions? And why preach moralisms about how we "should" and "must" and "ought" to love our neighbors, when we cannot have power to do that unless our selfish hearts are changed? Propositional and moralistic sermons both have one fault in common: They fail to mediate the actions of a saving Lord, because they fail to allow us to experience those actions for ourselves. They tell us *about* them; they never let us enter into them in the imaginations of our hearts.

By the same token, we cannot present the biblical story as something that has happened only in the past, recounting the event, and admiring God's marvelous deeds long ago, or even tacking on a few deduced applications to the present. If God's actions are not done now also for us through the sermon, they are of antiquarian interest only and are even goads to our hopelessness. God may have loved us once; the question is, Does he love us now? And is that love spelled out by his judging and saving deeds, which can give us a new beginning in our guilty and sin-worn world? The "plain style sermon," as James Cox names the form—the story in the past, then applied to the present—ignores the fact that the biblical story continues to exert its influence in the now.[2] No act of God in the Bible has been done only in the past. Through the medium of the biblical narrative, its effects continue into the present and impinge on our lives, for our weal or woe. Preachers handle "the living oracles of God" when they deal with the Bible. The words and form of the sermon must not ignore that present, shaping dynamism.

Finally, let it be emphasized again that if we want to be the heralds of the Bible's God and not of some other little godlets of our own devising, we cannot desert the biblical narrative and fly off into imaginative allegories, or even into modern parables and dramas supposedly more relevant than the Bible's story. The one Lord defines and reveals himself and acts through the biblical story, and we preach that story or we do not deal with *his* activity among us.

The goal of creative preaching is to tell God's words and deeds from the Bible in such a manner that the sermon becomes the medium through which those continue into the present, and we experience them, and they exert their saving influence on our lives. Such creativity does not begin merely at the point of applying the text, however. It begins with the initial act of exegeting the text, and it is to that task that we now turn.

GETTING THE STORY STRAIGHT: THE TASK OF EXEGESIS

There was once a student at seminary who objected to taking exegesis courses because it "ruined" his preaching. What he really objected to, of course, was having his homiletical thought shaped by something other than his own subjectivity. But that is the purpose of exegesis—to get at the actual story—to learn what it really says on its own terms and not what we think or wish it said. In other words, exegesis takes the Bible and history seriously. It acknowledges that the Bible is an objective "given"—a document with its own form and history and language and world-view and thought-world—and that the only way we can understand the Bible is by carefully investigating those phenomena with all the historical and scientific tools at our disposal. The Word of God has been spoken into actual history, to a real people, inhabiting a particular geographical location, speaking certain languages, within the framework of particular societies and cultures, and *it is that people* who has remembered and recounted and written down and passed on the Word to us in the canon of the Scriptures. The Word has been mediated to us through the earthen vessels of Israel and of the early church, just as we continue to mediate that Word to our people through the earthen vessels of our preaching (cf. II Cor. 4:7). To hear the Word, therefore, it is necessary to learn the languages in which it has been transmitted—Hebrew, Greek, and Aramaic; to study the way the Word has been preserved and passed on; to understand the historical and sociological and theological views in which it has been framed—in short, to know as fully as possible the particular situations and people to which the Word was first addressed and to probe the manner in which their ongoing history shaped the Word's form and content. God really did enter into actual human life, and real human beings mediated the story of his activity to later generations: Those are the facts that exegesis implies.

When we exegete, we start with a passage in the Bible in the original language in which it was transmitted to us. Because there are hundreds of varying manuscripts and manuscript traditions, we try to establish the most reliable reading of the text on the basis of the manuscript evidence and according to the laws of manuscript transmission.

Having established the best text possible, we translate the passage into English, conveying the meaning of the passage as closely as possible. In order to do that, we must consider word meaning, order, and function; the structure of the sentences in Hebrew or Greek, their emphases, the way they are related, and how the thought moves forward; where the climax of the passage is and what its subunits are.

We check the limits of the passage—where it begins and where it ends—marking off the boundaries of the passage by its internal unity, its coherence of thought, or its rhetorical and literary structure. We note the context of the passage and whether it could be removed from that context without disturbing the material around it.

Having established the unit we are studying, we turn to the nature of the passage.

We ask: Who put the unit in its present form? When? To whom was it addressed? And we begin to ask about the materials used in formulating the passage as we have it. What genre does the unit represent, and what was its original function and setting? Has that genre or form been changed, added to, or reduced? For what purpose have the changes been made? What is the function of the passage now? Is that function related to the larger context in which the passage is placed? How does the context affect the meaning of the passage?

Has the author or final redactor used older traditions in the passage? How has traditional material been used, and what was its source? Have changes been made in traditional material, and what is their purpose? Why has the author or redactor used such material? What does he or she want to say through it?

Are there parallel materials to the passage, or allusions, quotations, or comparable employments of words and thoughts in other parts of the Bible? Do these other materials throw additional light on the author's or redactor's intention and meaning in the passage? Or have the materials been used in a totally new way?

How are the historical and sociological setting of the author or redactor reflected in the passage? Are there anthropological, cosmological, or theological views reflected in the passage that come from that person's cultural milieu? How have those been dealt with, and why? Are the intention and meaning further illumined by all these factors?

Is the passage a part of a larger whole from the hand of the same author or final redactor? What function does it serve in the whole? Could the whole stand alone and retain its meaning? Does the meaning of the part depend on the meaning of the whole? How are the part and the whole related?

What is the meaning of the passage in relation to the total canonical context? Is the meaning unique in the canon? Does it need correction from the canon? Does it support and fill out dominant themes in the canon? How would the canon be changed in meaning if the passage were removed?

Such are some of the many questions we ask in exegesis of the Bible.

It is the temptation of some preachers—busy, impatient, untrained, or lazy—to shortcut this exegetical process and to let someone else do it for them. And to be sure, there are portions of the process for which all preachers must rely on someone else's work. Many no longer know Hebrew and Greek and must rely on a comparison of English versions. All must turn to histories and atlases, archaeological, anthropological, and sociological studies of the ancient Near East for scientific data. All are dependent on concordances, dictionaries, word-books, biblical theologies. All should read reliable commentaries on each biblical passage. Consequently, the library of every preacher should be kept up-to-date and studied and used to its fullest capacity.

The worst failing in exegesis is to shun all such scholarly study and to buy and use someone else's sermon outlines. Unfortunately, dozens of publishing houses put out such sermon "helps." But the preacher who uses them has not the foggiest notion whether what he preaches on the basis of them has any relation to the biblical passage in question or not. How can he? He has not studied that passage. Its meaning has never come clear to him. He has not made the Word his own. He has not the slightest chance therefore of communicating the Word of God to his people, and he would do them a favor if he quickly abandoned the pulpit altogether. Fortunately, there are not too many pulpiteers who engage in such dishonesty.

There are a good many preachers, however, who do almost no serious exegesis. Instead, they read and reread and ponder the meaning of a biblical passage in an English version, counting on their seminary training and general experience to guide their thought in the right direction. But because they have not plumbed the details of their text, such preachers do not know what that particular passage says, and as a result, their sermons often are general presentations of the gospel as a whole, sounding the same themes over and over, Sunday after Sunday, as the preacher draws from his steadily draining fund of theological experience and knowledge. It is usually such preachers who eventually run out of anything to say. It is also often such preachers who themselves are not being instructed and enabled to grow in sanctification and knowledge of God because they are not feasting on the details of the Word of God from which such growth is possible.

Along the same line, there are also preachers who will study a passage in English only for as long as it takes a sermon idea to be generated from it. They then unleash their imaginations and spin out sermons from their own ingenuity. A recent book on religious imagination has advocated just such a procedure:

> What happens in sermonizing? The text grabs your imagination in a vague way. You work to make the vagueness explicit. You sit before a blank sheet of paper and let the text call forth ideas, comments, humor, scholarship, personal notes, anything that may or may not be helpful. The imagination proceeds to unify the material around a theme, and prompts you to throw out 90 percent of the mental ramblings you have set down. The final product, the sermon, has as much imaginative thrust as you can include. It represents the total insides of you at that particular moment.[3]

It is not our own insides which we are called to proclaim, however, but the story of God's deeds and words, and this same book on religious imagination, further on in its argument, reveals that too often its methodology results in using the text as a pretext. If we do careful exegesis, there is nothing vague about the meaning of a biblical text. Rather, its principal thought, its setting, its intention, its function, and its theology are usually rather clear. It is the purpose of exegesis to make them clear, and those characteristics of the text uncovered by exegesis then become the controls for the content and shape of the sermon. We do not preach ourselves and our own imaginations from the pulpit. We preach the biblical message in an imaginative fashion.

Far too many preachers who *do* engage in the work of exegesis make a different mistake: They preach the views of the commentaries and not the message of the text. As inspiring as the writings of our

biblical scholars and theologians sometimes may be—and who
would want to do without the volumes from George Adam Smith or
Gerhard von Rad or Father Raymond Brown?—their words are
nevertheless not the Word of God, and they are not to be preached as
if they were. Their words are *about* the Bible, but their words are not
the biblical message. Such scholars may help illumine the biblical
text for us; they have no intention of replacing it. It is the text that
must speak to our gathered people, and it is we who must enable it to
do so; this means that when we have completed the initial tasks of
critical exegesis, we still will not have completed our preparations for
the construction of a sermon.

LISTENING TO THE TEXT

The next stage in exegesis is that of listening to the text, of
brooding over it, and of meditating and praying over it—ideally, over
an extended period of time—until the message we have uncovered in
exegetical study becomes the authoritative and acting Word of God
for us, spoken into our contemporary situation. We have got the
story straight. We have removed our preconceived notions about it.
We have eliminated the obstacles to understanding it in itself. We
have uncovered its central thrust and intention. The next step is for
the story to become our story.

Now at last we stand trembling behind our doors marked with
blood, our kneading bowls on our backs, our loins girded for flight,
while the wrath of the Lord passes over us, and we are delivered out of
death and slavery into new life and freedom (cf. Exod. 12). Now at
last we stand at the foot of Sinai, while the mountain burns with fire
and is wrapped in darkness, cloud, and gloom, and we hear the
sound of a voice, but we see no form; there is only the demand, "You
shall have no other gods besides me, for I am your savior from the
land of Egypt" (cf. Deut. 4:11-12; Hos. 13:4). Now finally we sit at
table and hear his grief, "One of you will betray me" (cf. Mark
14:18), and we stumble out into the night (cf. John 13:21-30), where
there prowls the devouring beast (cf. I Pet. 5:8). Here and now, we
cry out, "Have mercy on me, O God, according to thy steadfast

love!" (Ps. 51:1), and the One we have done to death nevertheless stands in our midst and forgives: "Peace be with you" (cf. John 20:19). And so it becomes our feet, beautiful upon the mountains, speeding to announce the good tidings of that which has happened to us—that God reigns (cf. Isa. 52:7), victorious Lord over all our evil betrayals and hopeless captivities and sinful sicknesses unto death.

It must be emphasized that the texts and stories of the Bible continue to speak in this fashion, if only we will not abandon them but will continue to listen to them and will not attempt to substitute our own words for them. By that I do not mean that we do not translate the language of the Bible into the language of today or that we do not draw analogies to our own life from the life of Israel and the New Testament church, but rather that it is the message of the text—and very often its figures of speech—from which we preach, and not some extraneous theme we have abstracted from the text or some topic we have imposed upon it.

The fact that the texts of the Bible continue to speak long after their original events have taken place, is constantly exhibited in the Scriptures themselves. For example, the event of the Exodus happened not only to that small mixed group of Habiru slaves who came out of Egypt, but was remembered in the liturgies of Exodus (cf. 12:42, 43-49; 13:3-16) and became the constituting act of God for every generation of Israelites thereafter. Apparently, the event originally was interpreted primarily in terms of Yahweh's power over nature, empires, and foreign gods (cf. JE), but Deuteronomy understood it primarily as the testimony to Yahweh's love and faithfulness (cf. 7:6-8), to which Israel was to respond in love. The preexilic prophets contrasted the witness to God's love and faithfulness in the deliverance from Egypt with Israel's harlotry and fickleness and thereby magnified the depths of her sin (cf. Amos 2:10; 3:1-2; Hos. 11:1-7). Second Isaiah interpreted the event as the prefigurement of Yahweh's final salvation of his people (Isa. 52:11-12) and compared it to the Lord's initial creation of the universe (51:9-11). Then the New Testament picked up the history and saw it recapitulated in the return of the holy family from Egypt (Matt. 2:14-15), but also primarily in the event of the cross (cf. Luke

9:31 ["departure" is literally "exodus"]; I Cor. 5:7-8; cf. John 19), and the act of God was understood not only as liberation from political slavery, but more profoundly as liberation from the slavery of sin and death. Thus the Lord's Supper became our passover celebration of the Exodus, preserving the canon's multiple themes of memorial, sinful betrayal, redemption, and eschatological expectation of final salvation (cf. Luke 22:14-23), as well as our entrance into the new covenant promised by the prophets (cf. I Cor. 11:23-26; Jer. 31:31-34; Heb. 10:11-17). The text, the original event of the Exodus, continued to exert its influence within the life of the people of God through all the years from about 1280 B.C. to A.D. 28 and on into the present situation of the church. And it is just such continuing, living action of the Word that preachers are called to proclaim.

It is noteworthy, in the example used, that the Exodus undergoes continual reinterpretation, depending upon the situation into which the Word is spoken. The original event is never lost, but it is seen in many different lights, and the case is no different when we speak the Word into our new situation. There, too, the event of the Exodus, to continue the example, is constantly reinterpreted in our preaching. For blacks, its liberation themes always have been primary, whether framed in terms of the spiritual's words to "let my people go," or by the identification of Martin Luther King, Jr., with a new Moses, or in the liberation theology of James Cone. For white suburban churchgoers, the message may be entirely different: Our slavery may have to do primarily with the tyranny of the self, or with the dead hand of principalities and powers of government, and the freedom announcement deals with those concrete enslavements; or perhaps some of us are the Egyptians in the story, oppressing our fellow human beings, and we must be confronted with the judgment of God on our ways. The point is that the text continues to speak, to illumine, and to act on us within our situation, and the preacher is the mediator and servant of that speech and action.

Because of this, the preacher must know not only the message of the text through and through, but also the situation into which the text is spoken. We not only exegete the biblical passage; we also must exegete daily the condition of our congregation. It will not do to view them as slaves, if in reality they are more like Pharaohs, nor will it do to treat them as Pharaohs if they are helpless slaves. Discerning that difference in the condition of our people is a full-time pastoral job.

In other words, the preacher not only listens to a text for himself or herself. He or she also engages in what Leander Keck has called priestly listening—that is, listening to the Word on behalf of the congregation, listening to its specific message for that specific community, at that particular time and place.[4] The message of a single text may be entirely different from year to year, as the situation of the people changes, and this is why we never can claim we know what the Bible says. We may know what it said last month, but what does it say this month? The Word continues to speak, or as Paul Scherer once pointed out, "God kept on talking after his book went to press."[5]

That is another reason we cannot rely on someone else's sermon outline or on the interpretation of some commentator. They have interpreted the message for their situation, but their situation is not ours, and the message of the text for our people may be entirely different from the message for theirs. This is also why it is unwise to use sermons from our "barrel." The situation of the people has changed, and the sermon has grown stale and out-of-date—that is, out-of-situation with the present condition of the congregation. The Word of God continues to speak ever afresh and anew, addressing the contemporary condition of God's gathered people. That, finally, is the reason the Bible's message cannot be reduced to "timeless truths." The Word comes at us like a two-edged sword, dissecting our condition and piercing to the bone and marrow of our life at the present moment.

The exegetical task is not finished until the preacher knows the condition of the congregation and hears the text, as exegeted, speak to that condition. And the preacher should not guess at the condition of the people, any more than he or she should guess at the meaning of the text. Visiting in members' homes and in their hospital rooms, listening to their conversations, paying attention to their comments during committee meetings, counseling, going to church suppers, taking part in every form of congregational activity—these are priceless exegetical opportunities, through which the alert preacher learns to know his or her people. Christ has made us "fishers of men" (Mark 1:17), and as George Eliot once remarked while listening to the complaints of some angling friends about the fruitlessness of their fishing, "You should make a deeper study of the subjectivity of the trout."[6]

In short, the meaning of a biblical passage is not contained solely within the Bible. It is found at the point where the biblical passage and the situation of the congregation meet—at the point of crux, of crossing, of crisis. The text interprets the situation; the situation shapes the interpretation. It is at that crucial juncture that the preacher must do the exegesis, and it is at that crisis point that the creative preacher must learn to hold text and situation in delicate balance. For example, no matter how oppressive the condition of the people to whom the exodus-redemption by God through the cross is proclaimed, it is a warping of the canon to limit that act to a political and economic liberation; the freed slave is quickly set under the moral demand of God, whether we are speaking in Old Testament terms or in those of the New (cf. I Cor. 5:7-8). On the other hand, it is equally a corruption of the biblical message to spiritualize the Exodus event; all parts of the Bible are concerned with the material and social and political needs of people. Thus while the situation into which the text is spoken helps determine the meaning of that text for the present congregation, there are limits set upon its interpretation by the limits of the canon; that means there are limits set upon the preacher's imaginative interpretation of the text. We dare not desert the biblical Word, for that is desertion of the Bible's God. Even as they continue to speak, the Scriptures stand as authoritative measure of our contemporary interpretation of them.

THE FINAL STEP: PASSION

It must not be assumed from what we have said about the preacher's exegesis of the congregation and the text that that study issues only in cold and scientific logic, in which people and Word are analyzed and brought neatly into juxtaposition. To be sure, the preacher must use all his or her scientific and critical and analytical skills in the task of exegesis; in many ways, biblical exegesis is a science, like other sciences. But there is more involved in being an interpreter of the Word of God than in other sciences, for finally, we are dealing with the love of God in Jesus Christ. And that love poured itself out in total identification with us. "He had to be made like his brethren in every respect" (Heb. 2:17).

> For he said, Surely they are my people . . .
>   and he became their Savior.
> In all their affliction he was afflicted,
>   and the angel of his presence saved them;
> in his love and in his pity he redeemed them;
>   he lifted them up and carried them all the days of old.
>   —Isaiah 63:8-9

Christ entered into our temptations, our hunger, our thirst; he shared our sorrow and our tears, and knew our abandonment and loneliness; he participated in our joy in friends and work and in our happiness in the beauties of nature and human companionship; he experienced our angers and frustrations as well as our satisfactions. Finally he bore our pain and entered into our death, and he became the first among us to be raised to newness of life. From birth to death, he shared our life, incarnating in his flesh that oneness with his sinful people of all the prophets before him (cf. *e.g.* Jer. 8:22-23).

God's love has always been so—hearing our cries (cf. Exod. 3:7), grieving over our wrongs (cf. Gen. 6:6), patiently going with us (cf. Exod. 33:14), tending to our needs (cf. Deut. 8:4-10), helping us to walk (cf. Hos. 11:1), shielding us from chaos (cf. Ps. 46)—everywhere living in our midst and encompassing us with a holy love that will not let us go (cf. Hos. 11:8-11).

Preachers, the "ambassadors" of God through whom he has chosen to make his appeal (II Cor. 5:20), therefore bear that message of total identification, and our very calling binds us up in the bundle of life with each and all of our people, in a holy love that yearns for them and grieves with them and rejoices with them (cf. Rom. 12:15). W. E. Sangster expressed it this way.

> To stand in the pulpit on a Sunday and see the eager and expectant faces of the people turned toward you . . . to feel, as you look at them, These are my people; to know that in all the great hours of their lives, when they want to be wed, when a child is born into their home, when trouble comes, when the doctor is going in and out, when bereavement robs them of every scrap of joy—to know that in such hours the door is open, and you not only may go but you must go; that the cry of their heart then is for their minister—to dwell upon that is to know a joy which, to my mind, not even the unquestioned delights of scholarly research can surpass. To receive the confidence of people; to know the secrets they have told to no other living soul; to blush with them over their sins and exult with them when the sin is flung under the table; to know their private affairs and to be the sharer of their highest ideals, is to have a joy of which not one of us is really worthy.[7]

We know our people finally, not because we analyze them, but because, to the depths of our being, we love them and care for them. That love has been prompted in us by the very Word we bear. There was once a minister-student who was having difficulty, not because he could not speak, but because he did not like his congregation. "They're a bunch of self-centered, egotistical jerks," he said, and he felt that he and God were fighting a losing battle over against his congregation. He failed to grasp that God in Christ was not on his side, but over there in the midst of the people, identifying totally with them. We must share that loving identification with our people or we have no part in Christ.

Such love cannot be faked, of course. Perhaps it rises first of all out of living with a people for so long that one comes to know deeply their terrible, terrible need. Each individual in every congregation is undergoing some sort of suffering. As the gospel described the people in Jesus' time, "When he saw the crowds, he had compassion for them, because they were harassed and helpless, like sheep without a shepherd" (Matt. 9:36). The people who fill our membership rolls really are no different.

Our love for our people also rises out of knowing, in the light of the

Word, that we are just as helpless and as needy as they are, and that people and pastor together are totally dependent on the love of God. As the great homiletician Thomas Chalmers once asked, "What could I do if God did not justify the ungodly?"

It is the passion, then—the passion of knowing that in the text on which we will preach to our beloved people next Sunday, there is healing for the hurt of some broken heart; life for the dying of one guilty soul; hope for the despair of some woman as she looks at the future; joy to replace the dullness of some man's jaded routine; peace for the divisions which wrack a home or community—that knowing finally gives exegesis fire which sets our hearts aflame with the message. It is what is at stake that makes the meeting of text and people so urgent, and knowing what is at stake is the crown of the exegetical endeavor. The apostle Paul knew. Singing out that marvelous persuasion that nothing could separate us from the love of God in Christ Jesus our Lord, he followed it with the terrible anguish, "I could wish that I myself were accursed and cut off from Christ for the sake of my brethren" (Rom. 8:38–9:2). Life—the life of victory in Christ—is offered to our people through the text. The passion to mediate that life, no matter what it costs us, is the fruit of true exegesis of our text and of our people.

IV. TEXT, SERMON FORM, AND CONGREGATIONAL IDENTIFICATION

The preacher stands at that crucial point where the exegeted text and the exegeted congregation meet—where the Word is heard by the preacher on behalf of the people as the Word for them. It is at this point that the preacher begins to shape the sermon as a whole, but until that whole is envisioned, the preacher should not begin to write the sermon.

Beginning homiletics students often make the mistake of starting to write when they have only a startling introduction or a good illustration or one point in mind. That is, they have part of a sermon idea, but they have not mastered their text in relation to their congregation, and they have no notion of how to proceed or how the sermon will end. The results are usually many hours wasted in fiddling with thoughts, writing, discarding, and rewriting, and an end product which more often than not fails to hang together or to affect the congregation, or even to voice the vague excitement the preacher felt when he or she started.

Shaping the sermon as a whole has often been discussed in terms of the "basic sermon idea," and the ideal has been pictured as the ability to set forth in one sentence across the top of a page what one desires to say. That method may state what one wishes to express, but it often has many shortcomings. First, it may ignore the text altogether or use it as a pretext. Second, it may take the text and turn its major thrust into an intellectual idea, thereby defeating the action of God at the start. Third, unless there are several modifying clauses in the sentence, it says nothing about how the idea will be developed; it therefore gives no notion of the form of the sermon. Fourth, it follows that there is nothing said about how the congregation will identify with the text. In short, the entire concentration is on content, apart from form and function, and sometimes even apart from the text. But all these elements in sermon-making go together, and unless the content of the *text* is expressed in a *form* that performs the desired *function*, the sermon will not communicate its intended message.

We have repeatedly stated that we want the biblical story of judgment and salvation to become our people's story. We want God's speaking and acting through the text to be speech and action done to and for them. Accordingly, we ask this crucial question when shaping the sermon as a whole: How can my people identify with this text? There is, moreover, no one answer to that question. There are many different forms a sermon may take in order to foster that identification; in order to allow the biblical story to become the story of our people's lives; in order to let what is at stake in the text become the burning issue of their living. And usually the form of sermon we choose in order to enable it to function in that manner grows out of the type and message of the text. Let us consider a range of possibilities in shaping a sermon as a whole.

STANDARD FORMS: THEMATIC AND PROCLAMATIONAL SERMONS

I think it fair to say that the majority of sermons preached in mainline churches in this country are thematic sermons. Wags have sometimes characterized such customary preaching as "three points and a poem," or "three points and a deathbed scene," noting that such sermons often move to what is intended to be a rousing or inspiring climax. Our people are so accustomed to hearing this form that when a preacher deviates from it, they often complain that they cannot follow the sermon. Such sermons are usually based upon a theme distilled from the text—worship, repentance, prayer, the love of God, faith, forgiveness, whatever— although in more aberrant examples, the theme is imposed on the text, or the text is ignored altogether. When the theme of the sermon concerns an issue of the day—race relations, marriage, war and peace, abortion, crime—the type is often called a topical sermon and may be related even more loosely to a text or texts. When the theme becomes a theological subject—sin, the judgment of God, the atonement, the sacraments—the product is often labeled "doctrinal," and very frequently the text is abandoned for a treatment of the gospel in general.

Such thematic sermons have traditionally been formed in one of several different ways. Some merely state a thesis and then support it with argumentation, evidence, and appeals to various authorities. In *The Twentieth-Century Pulpit*, G. Earl Guinn's sermon, "The Resurrection of Jesus," does this. Other sermons simply discuss a subject, as is true of James T. Cleland's "The Unattractiveness of Jesus." Some thematic sermons have been used to illumine a complete thought stated in the title of the sermon. For example, Harry Emerson Fosdick's presentation shows why "The Sacred and the Secular Are Inseparable." Some thematic sermons discuss a doctrine, as does D. M. Baillie's "The Doctrine of the Trinity." Some answer a question: Martin Luther King, Jr., deals with how evil can be cast out. When a thematic sermon becomes proclamational, it announces the Good News, as does Eduard Schweizer's magnificent presentation of "God's Inescapable Nearness."[1]

When you study these sermons, it becomes very clear that they all share substantially the same form, which can be rather easily outlined in terms of major points and subpoints. And yet the difficulty is that only the sermons by Baillie and Schweizer deal closely with their texts. Guinn's text from Romans 10:9-10 comes from a discussion by Paul of the difference between righteousness through the Law and righteousness through faith, in relation to the status of Israel; but this context is ignored and faith is equated with belief in the authenticity of the Gospel records. Cleland's text is from the "Suffering Servant Song" of Isaiah 52:13–53:12, but the theme is simply lifted out, with no examination of its meaning in the song. Fosdick's texts are not stated until the end of the sermon, and then the meanings in their contexts are totally ignored. King's text from Matthew 17:19 is more closely handled, but still the biblical narrative is treated only briefly. Baillie, on the other hand, takes one of the few Trinitarian formulations in the New Testament and illumines its meaning in a narrative style from the story, summing it up in a powerful statement of its meaning for us. Schweizer, appealing throughout his sermon to the situation of his hearers, proclaims God's nearness in Christ and shows his congregation what it means for them, basing each point on a major thought in the text.

In short, only those thematic sermons which derive their major points from the biblical material itself can lay claim to presenting the message of the text. The other sermons mentioned go entirely outside the Bible to find their points—to human experience, philosophy, church doctrine and creeds, poetry, scholars' findings, anecdotes, and quotes. It is not the message of the Bible that is being presented, but the sum of the preachers' learning and experience, and while the sermons are well shaped, they cannot claim to mediate the biblical story.

It is also significant in these thematic sermons that the more closely the preacher deals with the biblical material, the more narrative his style becomes, and the more the life of the people of God—whether that pictured in the Bible or that of the congregation—is portrayed in terms of action. Baillie's sermon deals almost entirely with the experience of the early Christians. Schweizer's treats the life of faith entirely as one of practice. The other sermons, by way of contrast, deal with ideas, opinions, and beliefs about this or that. The vital identification with the life mirrored in the text has been forfeited for thoughts *about* God and human existence. The gospel has become a static entity rather than a transforming experience.

It is a fact that the biblical message is framed for us largely in terms of narrative. Our salvation by God in Jesus Christ is a story, which reaches from Mesopotamia to the new Jerusalem, and even in those portions of the Bible where the message is phrased in affirmations and truths, the context is always the story of what God is speaking and doing in human life. It follows therefore that even a thematic sermon must preserve the dynamic character of the biblical record.

Finally, if the thematic sermon is to enable the biblical story to become our people's story, the congregation must be able to identify with it in some manner.

So we have three elements the preacher must consider in shaping a thematic sermon: (1) the meaning of the text, which (2) concerns a story, with which (3) our people must identify. How can we pay attention to all three elements—content, form, and function—at the same time, without tying ourselves in knots?

We cannot possibly do so if we formulate the sermon as thematic sermons usually have been formulated—that is, by taking a theme or a topic and expounding on it. That immediately locks us into static ideas; we usually will draw our points from outside the text, and we will then rely on extraneous illustrations and authorities to apply the points to the congregation.

Let us begin in a different fashion, treating the text as a whole within its context. Suppose we are preaching from Deuteronomy 30:15-20.

> I call heaven and earth to witness against you this day, that I have set before you life and death, blessing and curse; therefore choose life, that you and your descendants may live, loving the Lord your God, obeying his voice, and cleaving to him; for that means life to you and length of days, that you may dwell in the land.
>
> —verses 19-20

These are the words of Moses, addressed to Israel on the plain of Moab, according to the setting in Deuteronomy, shortly before Moses' death and Israel's entrance into the promised land, in the last quarter of the thirteenth century, B.C.

On first consideration, it would seem that we are dealing here with legalism and works righteousness, and the preacher is tempted to view the text as having nothing to do with justification by faith in Christ. As a matter of fact, however, a portion of Jesus' Sermon on the Mount closely parallels the thoughts of this text:

> Enter by the narrow gate; for the gate is wide and the way is easy, that leads to destruction, and those who enter by it are many. For the gate is narrow and the way is hard, that leads to life, and those who find it are few.
>
> —Matthew 7:13-14

There follow, in the Matthew passage, the warning to beware of false prophets and the statement that the sound tree can be known by its fruit. Then comes the saying, "Not every one who says to me, 'Lord, Lord,' shall enter the kingdom of heaven, but he who does the will of my Father who is in heaven." This is followed by the metaphor which states that he who hears Jesus' words and does them is like the wise man who built his house on the rock. In short, obedience, in both passages, issues in life for the believer.

This presents the preacher with another temptation—to construct a moralistic sermon, exhorting the congregation to faith and obedience. But an examination of the context of the Deuteronomic passage prevents this distortion. In Deuteronomy, Israel is pictured underway, midpoint between her redemption out of slavery and her entrance into the promised land and the final fulfillment of God's promises. She has already been redeemed and brought into relation with her God by his loving activity on her behalf: This is a point stressed again and again in Deuteronomy. She therefore is exhorted by Moses to respond to God's love by loving him in return and by cleaving to him—that is, she is to trust him totally with her life, give her heart to him, and therefore obey his voice. The context of the call for obedience is the grace that Yahweh has shown to Israel; the motivation of obedience is to be Israel's loving and grateful trust in response. The promise of the passage, then—for the pericope is promissory—is that such loving and obedient trust will issue in abundant life for Israel, symbolized always, in Deuteronomy, in terms of long life in the land.

This is also the message Jesus is speaking in Matthew: The motivation of the obedient life is love and trust in Jesus. As the Fourth Gospel puts it, "If you love me, you will keep my commandments" (John 14:15). And the outcome of such a life of love and trust and obedience is eternal life—abundant life, in company with God and fellow Christians (cf. John 3:36, 10:10, 17:21-24, et al.). In short, in these passages, both Old and New Testaments are saying that we do not automatically float down the stream of grace into our final salvation. We must respond to the redemption given by God, or we may lose the life which God so

much wants us to have, and for which he has sacrificed the very life
of his Son.

You will notice that I have not used the Deuteronomy text alone.
I have deliberately paired it with the Matthew text, and the reason is
theological: The Old Testament becomes addressed not only to the
Jews but also to us Christians, but only through the work of Jesus
Christ, who has made us the new "Israel of God" (Gal. 6:16); grafted
us as wild branches into the root of Israel (Rom. 11:17-24); made us
members of the commonwealth of Israel (Eph. 2:12-22); made us
heirs and offspring of Abraham (Gal. 3:29)—the New Testament
uses all sorts of figures. We become Israel in Jesus Christ, and thus
the Old Testament is addressed also to us, but only when we pair its
message with that of the New Testament. And it is precisely the Old
Testament passage which here illumines the meaning of the New
and which prevents us from a faulty interpretation.

We have briefly indicated the meaning of the texts in their
contexts. The question now becomes, How can we enable our
people to identify with this Deuteronomy text? How can its message,
which so illumines Jesus' teaching, become the Word for them?

It can do so by the method of analogy. We Christians have
become members of Israel, and so this is *our* story in Deuteronomy;
Israel's total situation there before God is remarkably parallel to our
total situation before him. We both are underway. We both have
been redeemed out of slavery. We both have not yet entered into our
final fulfillment. We both have a response asked of us by God. In
other words, if we deal with the *story* in Deuteronomy; if we do not
try to distill a "theme" out of the text, but rather ask what is going on
and what the action is, the message comes clear, and the sermon
almost writes itself. It has to do with our journey and our choice, and
its outline goes like this.

> Introduction: You and I are now on a journey through
> life, traveling somewhere between a time when we were
> enslaved and captive and a time when we shall enter into
> our final fulfillment and salvation.
> I.   So it was with Israel. . . . (the story briefly told)
>   This is the description of our lives, too. . . .

We may think our days are aimless wandering
from one thing to the next . . . (pictures)
We may think there is nothing behind us but our
own particular biographies . . . (pictures)
We may think there is nothing ahead but the
completion of some task . . . (pictures)
But the truth is that now you and I have moved out on
a fateful journey, traveling a road on which the Lord
God has set us in his purpose. And we were started on
the journey—on this soul-size pilgrimage—by being
rescued out of slavery by Jesus Christ . . .
slavery to death . . . (pictures)
slavery to evil . . . (pictures)
So the road we travel is now his road, leading from
redemption toward the future.

II. But that future depends largely now upon some
decisions we must make. Now we must practice
living as redeemed men and women. . . .
We can still fail to realize the full benefits of our
redemption . . .
That would be a terrible mistake to make, because
God in his love has planned such an abundant
future for us . . . (pictures)
But we must deliberately choose that life.

III. Our scripture lessons are quite convinced that we can
choose life only by falling in love with God. But they
are equally sure that we love God only by being
obedient to him. How else should it be?
Love is an action . . .
a living relationship . . .
a strenuous willing and effort to bring two lives
into harmony . . .
a day by day striving to communicate and share
and care . . .
the deliberate effort to walk along the same path
together . . .

This is the love we are to have for God . . .

It does not mean doing what is right in our own eyes—Israel lost her life doing that.

It involves obedience.

We begin to love and obey by . . .

trying to forgive others as God has forgiven us . . . (pictures)

caring for those for whom God cares . . . (pictures)

loving one another with the faithfulness God has shown toward us . . . (pictures).

IV.   We should have no illusions about what all this will cost—"The way is hard that leads to life."

Especially in our society . . . (pictures)

It takes single-minded concentration on his will . . .

vigorous exercise of self-discipline and firm decision . . .

consistent turning to God in prayer and worship and study of the Scriptures.

That is the meaning of cleaving to God, but then we will find ourselves in love with him.

Yes, it is hard to enter into life. But really, it is easy, too.

Who can help loving the God who has brought us thus far on our journey? . . . (pictures of what he has done).

Conclusion: So here we are, with that crucial decision before us—God holds out to us life and good and kindness and joy, in that fulfillment out there before us. "See," God says, "I set before you this day life and good, death and evil." And one can almost hear the great voice, resonant with love, pleading from the great heart of mercy, "O my people, choose life this day! O my people, choose life!"

Every major point in this sermon has come from the text, and the form has been developed out of the narrative context of the text: the picture of Israel now faced with the choice of life or death, as she is underway between her rescue out of slavery and her final fulfillment in the land. The congregation has a stake in the text from the very outset, because the story of Israel is made the story of their lives at the beginning of the sermon, through the method of analogy. Thus content, form, and function are all determined by the text. By concentrating on the whole text, in its contextual narrative setting, and not on some theme abstracted from it, the three aspects of the sermon are welded together.

There are other methods we may use to enable our people to identify with the text for a thematic sermon. Sometimes we are not dealing with the analogy between Israel and the church, but with the promise to Israel which is fulfilled in Christ. In that case, the identification with the text is made on the basis of the historical fact that we have become heirs of the promise and of its fulfillment.

There are some cautions we need to exercise in identifying with the Old Testament, however. First, a common error is to identify Israel with the United States, rather than with the church. But our nation, for all our love for her, is a pluralistic community which has never entered as a whole into the covenant with God through Jesus Christ. Indeed, for all our illusions about our idealism, we are a secular nation. It is the Christian church, not a national state, which Paul calls the Israel of God, and that church transcends all bounds of national, racial, ethnic, geographic, political, or sociological structure.

Second, it is a common error when dealing with the Old Testament to identify with its story or with some character in it, by means of allegory—that is, the characters and details of the story are made to stand for something or someone else. For example, the mark put on Cain's forehead is interpreted as the sign of the cross; the tent of meeting in the middle of the Israelite camp is equated with the village church in the center of the green in colonial America; Joseph, thrown into the pit by his brothers, is made a symbol of our struggle with evil; Jacob's ladder is seen as the stairway by which we mount toward heaven; or his "house of God" in Genesis 28:17 is identified with a local church building—all these allegories have been used in actual sermons. Sometimes sentences are removed from their context and made to apply to Jesus—for example, "Come in, O blessed of the Lord; why do you stand outside?" (Gen. 24:31) is paired with "Behold, I stand at the door and knock" (Rev. 3:20).

Preachers make these allegorical connections because they are not familiar enough with the Old Testament story and not creative enough to see the analogical connections between the history in the Old Testament and our history. But it is precisely a grasp of the story—of its character as "having happened"—that can prevent us from dissolving it into allegory and mere symbol.

For example, when preaching on the story of Jacob wrestling with the mysterious figure in the dark beside the ford of the River Jabbok, in Genesis 32, many simply dissolve Jacob into a symbol of our wrestling with God. But Jacob has a history attributed to him: the deception of his father Isaac and brother Esau; his flight to Laban in Mesopotamia; his receipt of God's promise; his fraud of Laban; his return to Palestine, during which the wrestling incident occurs; his meeting with Esau. It is in those occurrences that the revelation of God through Jacob's story takes place. The connection with our life, then, is analogical, and we must ask, How is Jacob's relationship with God, in his story, similar or parallel to our relationship with God, in our story? By hanging on to the character of the story of Jacob as "having happened," we prevent our turning it into an allegory, and we preserve the recognition that our story with God also actually happens; our faith is not dissolved into a fairy tale, having no relation to real events.

If we are dealing with a New Testament text apart from the Old Testament, once again we achieve identification with the biblical story through the method of analogy. Our lives and our situations in relation to God are seen to be analogous, or similar to the lives and situations of people and communities in relation to God in the New Testament. But as James Sanders has pointed out so cogently, we must be very careful to make the proper identifications in our interpretation of the New Testament text.[2] We love the parable of the prodigal son, with its unmerited grace, but we probably should usually be identified with the jealous elder brother. We liken ourselves to the disciples and put ourselves always on Jesus' side, so

that we become interested spectators of Jesus' offense to the
unbelievers around him, but usually we are like the scribes and
Pharisees; the priests and Levites passing by on the other side; the
Roman soldiers following orders; the officials afraid of the crowd; the
religionists shocked and disturbed by One who breaks all the rules
and who accepts subversives, prostitutes, and poor into the kingdom,
before us. It is largely our failure to draw the proper analogies that has
dulled the cutting edge of the gospel and that has turned the
radical message of the New Age in Christ into Sunday morning
"helpful hints for hurtful habits" (as Paul Scherer has phrased it).
Thus the gospel is prevented from coming to us as Good News,
because we feel we need only slight adjustments to be OK the way we
are. The message of our total dependence on God for life is stifled
under the certainty that we are free and that we really can accomplish
anything if we go all out in a crash program, supported by federal
funding. The biblical story is our story, but we must be careful to see
ourselves and our people in the proper persons and incidents.

OTHER SERMON FORMS

We have dealt at length with thematic sermons because they
represent the dominant form in American preaching today, but
there are other types of sermons which can be used effectively to
enable our people to identify with the biblical story.

There is the *narrative* form itself, in which we simply retell the
biblical story in vivid and imaginative language and let our people
enter into it. Human beings of all ages love good stories, and there
are some portions of the Bible that lend themselves admirably to
narrative sermons: the story of Jonah or that of Daniel—I have heard
both these done well—or the breath-stopping tale of Genesis 22.

If a biblical story is retold, the preacher must decide whether to let
the story stand by itself, to interpret it briefly, or to give a more
lengthy exposition of the meaning. Usually a lengthy exposition
ruins the effect of the story by breaking the mood of the
congregation's identification with it.

We also must realize that it is very difficult to tell a story well. As

Colin Morris has warned, "The narrative preacher had better be quite sure that he is not doing badly what the Bible has already done well—dragging out at tedious length in colourless speech what Jesus, for example, captured in one gripping anecdote or a few crisp sentences."[3] Narrative artistry is a skill not learned overnight. Most of the biblical stories have been polished and refined through years of transmission, and the preacher should approach their retelling with fear and trembling. There are also many problems involved. How can an Old Testament story be related to the New Testament? That relationship must be forged if our people are to become aware that we are dealing with events that concern them as the new Israel in Christ. Again, if the preacher retells a biblical story in his or her own language, the text must not be misinterpreted or psychologized or given details and meanings that are not in the Bible; the preacher may construct such a story, but it will not be the biblical story. Always, the text is the guiding measure and limit.

Closely related to the narrative sermon is the *running commentary*, in an earlier age called an expository sermon, in which the preacher moves through a biblical passage seriatim, interpreting as he goes. The Yahwistic materials in Genesis 2–11 have sometimes been used in this fashion, since they are intended to be pictures of every person's life. I do not think the parables of Jesus are properly employed in this way, however, since exposition of their separate details gives them meanings they were not intended to have. Billy Graham's sermon on the prodigal son is an example of the misinterpretations that can result.[4] Sagas, tales, and historical narratives from the Bible lend themselves much more readily to this form, but the running application of the text to the congregation must be very carefully done to avoid misinterpretations and a "shotgun" effect. Running commentary sermons often fail because they lack unity—meaning that the preacher has not seen the unity in the text.

There are also materials in the Bible—psalms, proverbs, some sayings and teachings—which lack any discernible historical context. That is, the preacher is confronted with texts from which he or she would like to preach, but they have no apparent story with which the congregation can identify. God has revealed himself through the Bible not only in deeds, but also in words, and sometimes those words have lost all their situational context. How then can the congregation be enabled to identify with them?

The identification can be made by showing how the words are our words or are directed to us in the midst of our Christian story. For want of a better title, we could call this a *word identification* sermon. For example, if we are preaching from Psalm 131, we enter into the thought of the psalmist and make his words ours, by showing how they are true in the midst of our Christian story: "I have calmed and quieted my soul, like a child quieted at its mother's breast." Or we take words from an Epistle and do the same: "I have fought the good fight, I have finished the race, I have kept the faith" (I Tim. 4:7)—surely that is our aspiration in the midst of our Christian living. Or we enter into Job's complaint: "Oh, that I were as in the months of old, as in the days when God watched over me" (29:2). Where the text itself has a situational context, we make that clear, but then by analogy, we show its meaning in the midst of our situation, which is "wound with mercy round and round as if with air."[5]

The point I want to emphasize, however, is that always there is a story involved—either the text's or ours, or both. We never dissolve the biblical message into timeless truths. The text's story has the quality of having happened, just as our story has happened in Jesus Christ and in his body the church, and by interpreting the text in those eventful contexts, we anchor its message to reality and prevent it from being a matter of indifference in our daily living.

The final form I might mention is that of the *evocative* sermon—a sermon which relies on indirection, suggestion, and questioning to prompt the congregation's identification with the text. This form is especially useful in dealing with texts which are surrounded by thick layers of mystery and which are therefore very difficult for the congregation to conceptualize and to identify with: eschatological portrayals of the New Age, visions, theophanies, or apocalyptic passages; texts dealing with life after death or with the being of God.

For example, there is no more telling challenge to the prideful powers of this world than the "taunt song" against the king of

Babylon in Isaiah 14:4-21, but the passage is crowded with ancient world images and mythological pictures, and no one should preach from such a passage in a direct fashion, as if reporting a historical happening. In the same manner, we should not ruin the images of the final resurrection in I Thessalonians 4:15-18 or I Corinthians 15:51-56, or of the appearance of God in Ezekiel 1 or Psalm 97:1-5 or Exodus 33:17-23, with clumsy attempts to literalize them. Nor should we take the visions of Daniel or of Revelation and try to correlate them with modern happenings. Through such texts, we are entering a world which "eye hath not seen nor ear heard"—a world of the mysteries of God—pictured for us by the biblical writers by intimation and poetry and symbol, and yet a world for which we long and which forms the goal of faith.

We therefore enable our congregation to identify with such texts by suggestion; by awaking the hungers of their hearts; by using images, as does the Bible, to hold out the certain hope that there will come a time when "God himself will be with them; he will wipe away every tear from their eyes, and death shall be no more, neither shall there be mourning nor crying nor pain any more, for the former things have passed away" (Rev. 21:3-4). The images are very concrete, touching the real human condition, and the certainty of such future is made secure by the story which has already happened. But the full mystery that awaits us is yet unknown—"now we see in a mirror dimly"—and we cannot literalize our images of it. We only know that when it comes, it will be full of the love of Christ.

Perhaps the best illustration of such an evocative sermon is Frederick Buechner's "The Hungering Dark."[6] He takes all our hopes and longings for God's future and makes us desire that future even more, and that evocation strengthens our faith and the possibility of our living in the present.

To sum up, the shaping of a sermon depends on the nature of the text one is treating and the ways the congregation can be enabled to identify with that text. Involved in the shaping are content, form, and function—all growing out of the exegeted biblical passage which the preacher hears speaking to him and to which he listens on behalf of his people.

V. EXPERIMENTAL SERMON FORMS

No book on creative preaching should ignore the many experimental sermon forms being tried out on congregations throughout this country. In fact, for some people, creative preaching is experimental preaching, though I would not concur in that identification. But there are many departures, sometimes very radical departures, being made from the standard church scene—a congregation sitting in pews, listening to a preacher deliver a Sunday morning sermon from a pulpit.

The reasons for the appearance of experimental preaching are many. During the desperate decade of the 1960s, preaching was considered by many activist clergy and laity to be passé. God, it was thought, was no longer present in his church in local congregations, mediating his grace to his people through the traditional means of Sacrament and Word. Rather, ran the theological rationale, God had shifted his locale and was present only in the world, working out his purpose especially among the poor and dispossessed and persecuted. Therefore, if the church wanted to know God, it was necessary for it to move out into the world, because it no longer could find God in its gathering, but only in its dispersion. Confronted with such a devaluation of the local church's traditional worship, some preachers turned to experimental forms of preaching, to provide at least some means of reflection and commentary on their congregations' activity in the world.

Fortunately, we learned from the experience of the 1960s that no social gospel can be sustained without the empowerment and foundations for it in the worship and proclamation of the local congregation. It can now be said that preaching is undergoing a renaissance in this country.

Yet some clergy still remain dissatisfied or discouraged with the preaching ministry. Some feel that traditional forms of preaching turn the congregation into passive spectators of a preacher raised on high and thus deny the unity of the church and the New Testament characterization of worship as the work of the people. Many feel that it is much too difficult to try always to preach from a biblical text. The Bible is so foreign to our secularized congregations that it takes too much time to explain a text and to bridge the gap between the Bible's world and that of the congregation. Or even when the bridge is constructed, the Bible's message, from a primitive and agricultural age, may remain irrelevant to our modern technological time. Not a few have observed that traditional forms of preaching never seem to affect their people or to draw new members into the church. The minister preaches and preaches, but the people do not change their ways of living, the membership roles are not enlarged, and the minister becomes convinced that standard forms of preaching are not the way to alter life-styles in the 1980s.

Out of all these frustrations and convictions, experimental preaching has been born, and it is now possible to find, at some place in the land, almost any type of homiletical or nonhomiletical event taking place at 11:00 A.M. or at 9:30 A.M. on Sunday morning, or at 7:30 P.M. on Wednesday evening, as a replacement for the traditional sermon. There are dialogue and multilogue sermons of all types—a clergyman/ventriloquist in Detroit even preaches in a dialogue with his dummy![1] There are first-person sermons, congregationally formed sermons, dramatic presentations of every kind, nonbiblical narrative readings, sermons accompanied by all sorts of visual and audio aids. The list of types of experimental preaching is almost as limitless as the human imagination.

Before we discuss these various forms of experimental preaching, however, let it be said very clearly: There is no substitute for the traditional preaching ministry of the church. Indeed, the church exists only where the Word is truly preached and the Sacraments are rightly administered. There is, by the promise of God, no tool more effective for creating and sustaining the life of the people of God than a well-delivered, well-shaped, proclamational sermon from a well-exegeted biblical text. Far too many preachers have turned to gimmickry in the pulpit because they are unwilling to expend the discipline, thought, and labor necessary to master their craft.

WHY THE EXPERIMENT?

If preachers wish to use experimental presentations, therefore, they should first do a lot of very deep soul-searching. They should ask themselves, Why am I using this experimental form? Am I doing so just to be faddish? We occasionally attend a small rural church near our vacation site in Pennsylvania. It is a relatively poor congregation, and the pastor is inevitably a recent seminary graduate. I shall never forget the Sunday the fledgling preacher and his wife subjected that congregation of farmers, shopkeepers, and small-town housewives to a folk song with what seemed like interminable verses, out of the youth culture of the 1960s, the whole delivered in the nasal twang of so many folk singers, to guitar accompaniment. Nothing could have been more alien to that congregation or more ineffective in presenting the gospel! But the clergy people thought they were being relevant and up-to-date.

As Colin Morris has commented,

> Whilst I admire the courage and imaginativeness of those persons or groups of laity who put tremendous effort and dedication into the task of livening up moribund church services in an honourable attempt to attract outsiders, I am afraid their liturgical innovations often go just far enough to irritate the faithful but not far enough to ensnare the godless.[2]

There must be some understanding and expectation of experimental forms created in the congregation before those forms can be used with any effectiveness whatsoever. Otherwise, the members of the church are alienated, and the unchurched see nothing about the body of Christ which is different from the expressions of the culture around them.

This brings us to the second question the experimenting preacher should ask: Do these new forms communicate the gospel better than did the old? So often the new forms are imported from campus cultures quite different from that of the average congregation, and their new modes and content of expression are as foreign, or more foreign, to the church's people than are the culture and expressions of the Bible. The preacher therefore is gaining nothing by using an experimental form. Henry Mitchell has said it well:

> The folk masses and the less-structured services which I have encountered all over the country are so sterile because they have no authentic root in previous culture. Things done on a drawing board cannot speak to the depths of personhood in worship, unless they take seriously and plug into what is already there.[3]

A preacher must take into account the context of the people, in order not to impose totally foreign expressions upon them.

The preacher also should ask if the use of an experimental form is simply an avenue for displaying a talent undisplayable to the congregation in any other way. Singing, guitar playing, dramatic reading, drawing, magic, instrumental music, ventriloquism—all these have been used by preachers in their sermons, or in place of them, but it is a question of whether the preacher wants to put on a performance or communicate the gospel. Paul Scherer, one of the greatest preachers of the past generation, was a skilled Shakespearean actor, but he did not preach the bard from the pulpit or engage in dramatic performance. He lost himself in the service of the gospel and subordinated all to Jesus Christ and him crucified. Our people's hunger always is, "Sir, we wish to see Jesus."

Thus the principal question every experimenting preacher always should ask is: Am I communicating the biblical story, and am I doing it in a manner that will enable the congregation to identify with that story? Reinhold Niebuhr regularly liked to discuss ethical and social issues relating to the growth of the auto industry with the people in his parish in Detroit. But he also confined that free-wheeling discussion to Sunday evening meetings, and he did not call it preaching or conduct it from the pulpit. George Buttrick, every Sunday evening, used to give what he called book sermons from his pulpit in the Madison Avenue Presbyterian Church in New York City, in an effort to put the people's reading into the context of the gospel and to bring the insights of notable authors to their attention. But Buttrick carefully related every book discussed to a scriptural text, and he always set it in the discriminating light of the Word of God. Christian preachers are entrusted with the biblical Word. We are "servants of Christ and stewards of the mysteries of God. Moreover it is required of stewards that they be found trustworthy" (I Cor. 4:1-2). The experimenting preacher always needs to ask if he or she is a faithful steward, keeping the Word and passing it on.

TYPES OF EXPERIMENTAL SERMONS

I cannot begin to discuss here all the details of the various experimental sermon forms being employed in this country. However, I can put together some rather broad categories of the types being used, in an effort to give some indication of the possibilities open to the preacher.

One of the most frequently tried forms is the *dialogue or multilogue* sermon, and there is now a good deal of literature dealing with this type. Sometimes such dialogue sermons are presented from the chancel by co-ministers of the congregation, or by a Roman Catholic and a Protestant, or by a Christian and a Jew. Sometimes the dialogue is carried on between clergy and laity, clergy and youth, clergy and skeptic, laity and laity. The purpose of such dialogue can vary. Sometimes it seeks simply to present varying views on a scripture text or a topic of the day. Or it can be used to uncover questions and their answers. Or it can bring two opposing points of view into friendly but thought-provoking conflict.[4]

Certainly a dialogue sermon can arouse a good deal of interest among the members of the congregation. If it is well done, it can give voice to previously unexpressed questions and issues hidden in the minds of the congregation and allow them, through identification with one or another of the speakers, to work their way through to answers and stances they otherwise might not have considered. Such sermons must be very carefully prepared to mirror the real positions of the hearers, and their presentation must be natural and spontaneous. If a dialogue sermon were to be really unstaged and authentic, it would be an extemporaneous presentation between two agile-minded and biblically grounded, articulate and irenic, mature and secure persons, but it is very difficult to find such participants, and most dialogues have the staleness of artificiality about them. Worst of all, most are little more than planned discussions having no relation to the biblical story, and while they may raise issues upon which the congregation may reflect—not a bad goal to be sure!—they are not substitutes for a biblical sermon. If there is to be a dialogue sermon, it should be based on a biblical text.

There are also various kinds of dialogue and multilogue sermons of the *congregational* type. Some preachers plant a person in the congregation to interrupt the sermon at midpoint and to begin a dialogue with it, although this sometimes shocks a congregation so thoroughly that they never recover sufficiently from their vicarious embarrassment to listen to what is being said. Other preachers give a brief message and then invite questions and discussions from the congregation, usually prompting one or two individuals ahead of time to get the discussion going. Or preachers will present a case study and invite congregational comment on it. Congregations also have been asked to complete phrases such as "Jesus Christ is . . ." or "Life in faith means . . ." and thus work out their own spontaneous sermons. Another form of congregational multilogue is the press-conference sermon, in which the congregation asks written or oral questions of the minister, but this tends to turn the minister into an "answer man."

The advantages of the congregational multilogue sermon are that it overcomes the spectator mentality, personalizes worship, emphasizes the importance of individual response to the gospel, and expresses the priesthood of all believers.[5] And preachers should not defeat such gains by insisting on their own positions in the discussion, or by preaching another sermon at the end—the discussion is intended to be the sermon. Obviously, however, one can never be quite sure just what direction the discussion will take, and it often can roam far afield of any Christian position. For this reason, it would probably be better if the congregational discussion were centered around a biblical text: What does the text mean to the people in their daily living? The minister can give a brief exegesis before the discussion begins, to clear away any misunderstandings of the text's historical setting and theological thrust. The task of the congregation is then to apply the text to themselves. One also needs to guard against one or two members of the congregation monopolizing the discussion or using it as a weapon against another person. It must be impressed upon the congregation that Bengel's rule should be theirs: Apply all thy powers to the text, and all its meaning apply to thyself.

Another frequently used form of experimental preaching is that of the *first-person* sermon. Usually the preacher assumes the role of a biblical character and speaks on behalf of that character, giving his or her thoughts and reactions to some situation in the biblical history. This type has become one frequently used at midweek Lenten services to portray the reactions of various biblical personages to the events of Jesus' passion. Frederick Speakman's "What Pilate Said One Midnight" is just such a sermon, while Peter Marshall's "The Rock That Moved" is a very imaginative variation on the type. [6]

The curse of such first-person biblical sermons is their misuse of the text. Unless extremely well done on the basis of sound historical and exegetical study, they inevitably psychologize the text, adding details never meant to be there, and thus introducing elements which alter and misinterpret the biblical passage. When dealing with a character in the Gospels, they also almost inevitably harmonize the Gospel accounts, covering over the particular theologies of the separate evangelists. Redaction criticism has gone to a good deal of trouble to isolate the unique theologies of each of the Gospel writers; first-person sermons should not ignore the fruits of that scholarly endeavor, because such ignorance blunts the witness to Christ, as given in the Gospel accounts.

It is also a fact that some preachers substitute the subjectivity of first-person sermons for hard study of the biblical record. It is not difficult to let one's imagination run wild. It *is* difficult to research the concrete details of the historical situation of Peter or Paul or some other biblical character, and then to use those as the details of the sermon. But only if such research is done should a first-person sermon be attempted.

The other form of first-person sermon being used rather widely is that of *personal testimony,* in which the preacher witnesses to what God has done in his or her life. The sermons by Theodore P. Ferris and John Killinger are examples.[7] Normally in preaching, we keep ourselves in the background, because it is not ourselves we preach, but Jesus Christ as Lord. Thus "I," "I think" or "I believe," "It is my opinion" or "It seems to me," are words and phrases we deliberately try to avoid, because they usually signal that we are speaking "as one of the scribes"—on our own authority and not from the authority of the text. We are not the saviors of our people; the Word of God in Jesus Christ alone is powerful and effective to save. But there does come a time occasionally when the faithful preacher goes through an experience or has his or her life so altered by the Word that he or she must declare, "This is what God has done for me." Then such personal testimony may powerfully transmit the biblical faith. However, such personal confessions should be sparingly used, for our principal task is to listen to the text on behalf of our people. It is what God is doing among them through his Word that is our subject, not what he has done to us alone from among his gathered congregation. Personal testimonies, if overused, can become occasions of spiritual pride and self-glorification, ignoring entirely the context of the church. It is precisely this individualistic, self-glorifying testimony that characterizes so many of the evangelistic TV and radio preachers of our time. Any message that ignores the body of Christ is not the gospel. The Word of God comes from and must be lived out in concrete community.

There are also many *dramatic forms* of experimental preaching being tried. These are presentations in which the preacher, and/or others, assume a role. Actually the first-person biblical sermon is a dramatic form, but we included it in the previous category because of customary labeling. Dramatic forms may also be in the shape of dialogues: between two biblical characters; between Christ and Satan; between the sheep and the goats—the "ins" and "outs" of our society; between the preacher and his alter ego, and so on. A multilogue of this type might portray an atheist, a pillar of the church, and a young person; or an environmentalist, a businessman, a government official, and a Christian. The possibilities for role-playing are almost endless.

Sometimes dramatic sermons are done in the form of oral readings by an individual or a group and can be very powerful if well written and well performed. Some preachers use verse sermons, or sermons in the form of letters read aloud; occasionally a preacher with a dramatic flair will act out a two-person drama, assuming both parts by varying the voice and stance.

There are also a number of experiments taking place with *mime and symbolic action and dance*. These are often silent, but they should not be, since they do not carry automatic meanings in themselves. Scripture readings should always accompany them to give their true focus. When this is done, sacred dance, for example, can be a very forceful expression, and congregations also have been asked to participate, with hand and arm movements or through word or song.

At times, *drama* as such has been used to replace the sermon altogether, and there have been some very powerful plays written for a chancel or church setting—for instance, Christopher Fry's *A Sleep of Prisoners*.

These forms of dramatic presentation should be used sparingly, and they never should be employed unless they are almost professionally done. Nothing is worse than a verse-sermon employing bad and subjective poetry, or a dance by a self-conscious and clumsy ballet student, or a drama in which the characters forget their lines. Let the church employ excellence to glorify God and not profane his holy name! But we do have some artists in the Christian church and among the ranks of the clergy, and their artistic talents can *occasionally* be used to the service of the gospel.

There are, further, *narrative forms* of experimental preaching in which the preacher tells a story or parable or allegory not taken from the Scriptures. One of the most effective sermons ever preached was that of the prophet Nathan to David, in II Samuel 12:1-7, with its point thrust home in the one-line application, "You are the man!" I do think that our sermons of this type should have the scripture lesson read alongside them as the context for the evaluation and application of the narrative, but whether or not the preacher explicitly connects the scripture text with the narrative depends entirely on the artistic demands of the situation. Sometimes it is better to let the congregation draw its own conclusions.

Now and then preachers will read the Scriptures alternately with headlines or brief reports from the daily newspaper, a device which may be effective in illuminating our darkness with the light of the Word. One of the most effective pentecostal preachers of our time, James Forbes, occasionally forms a sermon by taking the words of a hymn for his text. Some preachers have used the words from popular music or from a musical, in counterpoint to a scripture passage— some lyrics from the Beatles' music or from *Jesus Christ Superstar* are startling in the insights they afford into the biblical message. I myself have used Browning's poem, "Christmas Eve," as a running accompaniment to a scripture passage, in a brief chapel homily, but I would not use any of these devices very often. Headlines, hymns, music lyrics, and poems are better employed simply as illustrative materials in a sermon, rather than as dominant portions of it. Always, always, our responsibility is to that biblical Word.

There have been a number of experiments using *visual and auditory aids* in connection with the sermon. Some talented clergy/artists have given chalk talks as sermons, and I have seen felt boards used in small churches to illustrate a message. Thompson and Bennett report that one preacher gave a dialogue sermon with the organ, and I once witnessed a Sunday evening service in which various passages of scripture were punctuated, emphasized, and interpreted by the percussion section of a symphony orchestra, although it became clear about halfway through the program that the instrumentalists did not understand the scripture; this is always a danger when employing the talents of artists who have not first engaged in biblical exegesis!

Religious Media Today reported some time ago that some preachers are using slides to project the text of their sermons on screens beside the pulpits, along with outlines of the sermons as they progress.[8] But it seems to me that this would largely defeat any artistry of the sermon and reduce it to a cut-and-dried, rationalistic presentation. If our purpose is to preach to the ear, let us learn to do it effectively, so that words create such images in the minds of our congregations that they do not need accompanying written words.

Along the same line, preachers have occasionally used overhead projectors or colored slides of religious or other graphic art or architecture to substitute for spoken words, but they are assuming that nonverbal images and symbols convey a clearly defined message—an assumption that cannot be taken for granted. There is a real question whether there is any common artistic symbolism present in the country today, or even whether the artists themselves would sanction such use of their work.

Finally, there are dozens of *folk masses and religious musical dramas and testimonials* being produced today, just as there are dozens of *oratorios and masses and passions* from the pens of the great musicians of the past. These can aid the preaching of the church; William Holladay has recently pointed out that the principal interpreter of the Book of Isaiah for the modern church has been Handel's oratorio *Messiah*.[9] Alongside such interpretations, however, there always must be the ongoing proclamation of the Word, given by the preacher for that particular congregation. While an oratorio or folk mass might be used in place of the sermon once a year, such programs are better relegated to times other than 11:00 on Sunday morning. They can supplement the preaching of the church; they can never replace it.

If we do use experimental preaching in the church, we must take care always to ask for feedback from the congregation. What is the message that is being conveyed? What function is it performing? Is it communicating the biblical story and enabling our people to identify with that story?

Perhaps the chief error in the use of experimental forms in the church has been the notion that because some event takes place on Sunday morning in the time slot allotted for the sermon, it therefore is a sermon. But that is to use the word "sermon" far too loosely. A discussion group or a dialogue concerned solely with a topic of current interest is not a sermon, any more than is an uninterpreted mime or dance. A sermon is an oral interpretation of God's Word to his gathered people, through which he speaks and acts upon their lives. By that definition, many of our standard presentations on Sunday morning are not sermons, either. Sometimes God does not wish to act through our preaching; we can only pray that he will. More often than not, the fault is ours, and we stand in his way. But above all, we must remember that we have to do with the biblical story, and if an experimental form does not in some manner present that story or point to it, then we should leave that form to someone else and get back to our calling. We are entrusted with the biblical Word. As Paul once declared, "Necessity is laid upon me. Woe to me if I do not preach the gospel!" (I Cor. 9:16).

VI. LOGIC AND STYLE

After the preacher has done the work of exegesis of both text and congregation and has decided on the best sermon form for enabling the congregation to identify with the biblical story, he or she has the task of writing the sermon. It should first be set down in outline form—that aids the logic of the whole. Then it should be written out in complete manuscript form—that is the guard of style.

THE LOGIC OF IT ALL

It is a mysterious but nevertheless constantly recurring fact that many preachers have difficulty preparing sermons because they do not think in a straight line. That is, they do not develop a sermon as a unified and logical whole. They repeat points; they wander off on tangents; they introduce new thoughts or texts at the very end; they have two or three different sermons all mixed together. The result is that while their congregations may enter into the sermon at one isolated point or another, they are quickly sidetracked and are never allowed to experience the whole event of the text. The biblical story never becomes their story, because it is never presented to them as a logical whole.

In listening to an oral communication, the hearers must experience some logical progression in the presentation's thought and structure. One point must follow naturally and smoothly into the next, and the transitional phrases used must aid that movement.

Each separate paragraph must have an internal unity and each must belong at a natural place in the unified whole. Where contrasting paragraphs join, the transition between them must signal a logical shift. And the whole must have a definite beginning and ending. That all sounds very simple, but there are countless preachers who have not mastered such simplicity, and one of the basic differences between good sermons and bad has to do precisely with logic.

The best cure for illogical structure is the full sermon outline. Many seminary homiletics courses do not require the discipline of outlining, preferring to deal with "thought units" arranged into "moves," in the attempt to get away from sermons that turn the gospel into abstract ideas. But every story, every artistic expression, every oral presentation more than one word long has a structure. That is true even in unstructured modern art and drama, and until we grasp or are grasped by the structure, we really do not understand the expressions. For example, one of the differences between Schoenberg's music and that of a kitten on the keys is precisely structure. It is by fully and carefully outlining the sermon that the preacher can master structure. The outline will show immediately if there are any repetitions; if points follow in a logical sequence; if anything has been omitted or if extraneous thoughts have been introduced; if the whole hangs together. No sermon really can be analyzed fully until its outline has been uncovered. No sermon will be a good sermon until it has an internal logic. We will save ourselves hours of work and our congregations much confusion of mind if we will accept the discipline of first outlining our presentations.

In constructing the sermon outline, we must pay attention to its *movement*. Sermons never should allow the congregation, in identifying with the biblical story, to remain at a standstill too long. In their minds' eye, they should be constantly moving along—never doubling back on their tracks; never marking time at a way station already fully explored; always pressing forward toward a resolution, a goal, a climax—sometimes slowly, sometimes rapidly, but always in a steady movement. To be sure, they may be allowed to catch their breath occasionally with the pause afforded by an illustration, but they should not be led down a side path, never to return to the main road. When they arrive at the goal, they should retain a clear idea of where they started, where they have been, and where they have ended. They should be able to recount the course of the "journey" to a friend.

When you begin your sermon with an *introduction*, do not start the congregation off in a false direction. It is amazing how many preachers begin a sermon with a story or an illustration or a thought they want to express and then stray off in an entirely different direction in the body of the sermon. Also, start the congregation moving immediately: In the introduction, show them that they are underway—that this eventful journey in company with the living Lord is their journey—and then lead them out onto the main road as quickly as possible. The introduction should rarely be more than a half page in a double-spaced manuscript. If it is longer, the congregation begins to wonder where on earth you are taking them, or indeed, if you and they are going anywhere at all.

At the *conclusion* of the sermon, sum up the journey and drive home its reason and purpose, but do not introduce new ideas, new biblical texts, new directions. These give the congregation the feeling that the trip is not complete, that they missed something along the way, or that they are preparing to start out once again. Bring the movement to a definite end—do not halt it in fits and starts; give the impression that the final destination has been reached. Leave the congregation with the desired response on their lips and the wished-for resolve in their lives. Frame the conclusion in such a way that the people will respond appropriately to God—in praise, in prayer, in faith, in renewed dedication, in repentance, in awe, in ethical resolve—whatever has been the goal of the sermon, end it in a way that will prompt that response. Do not end on a negative note, or even with a question. Affirm, proclaim, evoke the reaction your people are to have, so that their final inward answer to the action of God mediated through the sermon is, "Yes, yes. Oh yes!"

A STYLE OF YOUR OWN

Having outlined with an eye to structure, logic, movement, and unity, the preacher now is ready to write out the sermon in full manuscript form, and once again there is no substitute for that particular discipline. Our language will not be the means of allowing identification with the biblical story unless it is carefully and deliberately chosen and shaped with an eye to that purpose. It must be simple and clear, expressing exactly what we mean. It must be concrete and pictorial, working on the imaginations of our people's hearts. It must be appropriate and beautiful, worthy to mirror God's glory. Unless we are geniuses with the spoken word, none of us can produce such language extemporaneously. It must be painstakingly thought out and written in full and complete form. We may then preach from notes or from an outline if we wish, but the language should be embedded in our minds. It must first be written down and the phrases and expressions absorbed, so that they flow forth automatically in the delivery of the sermon—not from memory, but from becoming our natural manner of expression for that particular sermon on that specific occasion.

Let me emphasize, however, that each person has his or her own style, and that no one should try to copy the writing or speaking style of another. I once heard a preacher who copied the aphoristic style of George Buttrick, right down to the stutter during delivery. It was a perfect imitation, but it was not an honest expression. We do absorb something of others' styles from our reading, of course, and if we read the works of great writers, the absorption helps improve our own style. But each of us has our own phraseology and vocabulary and rhythm and mode of expression, and we should work to improve our own style, not to copy another's.

For example, most books on preaching advise us, in writing our sermons, not to use long sentences. Sometimes that is good advice, but most of the time it is not, because the length of sentence one is able to handle depends almost entirely on one's speaking ability. Some speakers cannot meaningfully intone a sentence with more than two clauses. Others can write a very long sentence, with all sorts of modifying clauses, and make it crystal clear to their listeners through timing and inflection. If you will read the first sentence of Paul Scherer's sermon, you will find that it is eight lines long, with seven commas and a semicolon, but Scherer, a masterful orator, had

no difficulty in speaking that sentence clearly. Many of the
sentences in James Stewart's sermon are equally long, yet
Stewart was probably the greatest preacher of the past generation.[1]
The point is that they could speak well, and they wrote to match
their speaking ability. We must learn to do the same. If nothing
comes over clearly unless you put it in very short sentences, then
above all, keep your sentences short. If you can soar in your
speaking and handle a phrase and sustain a thought for eight lines,
then do not worry about the length of your sentences. Your style is
your own. The main thing is that your congregation should
understand each sentence.

You will want to vary the length of the sentences you use,
however, and that variation is done primarily for emphasis. Consider
the following extract from a sermon about death:

> The final, last insult to all the aspirations of the human personality; the
> great leveller of all our claims to pomp and glory; the inevitable end of
> every good dream and every loving relationship, death has held human
> beings captive, in fear, to its tyrannical void and oblivion. And try as we
> will to escape its clutches, we never can outrun its grasp or loose its cold
> fingers from encircling our lives and the lives of all whom we love. We
> cannot. But God did, in the resurrection of Jesus Christ.[2]

The thought flows along until the main point is reached. Then there
is a sentence with two short words, followed in the next sentence by
three short words in the clause and the resolution of the problem. It is
not difficult to speak that phraseology and to put the emphasis in the
right place; the language is structured in such a way that the
emphasis is written into it.

I am not sure anyone can consciously learn the rhythms of the
English language so that phrases occur at just the right points and the
emphases are clearly apparent. Everyone has his or her own rhythm
of speech, and you must adhere to your rhythms, or your speech will
sound artificial and contrived and indeed, will be so. You must learn
to feel the rhythm of your own words deep in your self and then write
your manuscript to adhere to those rhythms, so that they may be
recaptured orally when you deliver the sermon. The congregation is

then carried along by the rhythms, is caught up in them, and thus is aided in "living into" the sermon.

There should be variation in your rhythm. If you always write and speak in choppy sentences, you will soon annoy your congregation; if you only flow freely along, the people will not grasp the most important points. But perhaps varied rhythm is absorbed into your bones by reading the fine writing of others; then you take pains to write into your manuscript the meter which you sense.

I think style actually is a matter of the heart. When the heart is engaged, words flow naturally in a pleasing rhythm. For example, it has been shown that poetry was the instinctive language of emotion for ancient peoples, and it is no accident that the majority of the prophets framed their oracles in poetic structures. When the heart is engaged, words also become concrete and pictorial. For example, if you are angry at someone, you do not express your irritation in abstractions; you tell that person precisely how you feel, and not infrequently, your words are very vivid. The secret of style in preaching is the engaged heart of the preacher—that passion to communicate the Word one has heard to one's beloved people.

Let us put it another way. Style is the man! Or the woman! As you are, in your own meeting with the Word of God on behalf of your people, so your style will be as you speak from the pulpit. For example, all preaching should be in *simple* everyday words, which are absolutely *clear* to the congregation, but whether that is the case often depends on the pride and ego of the preacher. Does he want to show off his learning and erudition? Does she want to exhibit her grasp of profundities of thought? The more that is true, the longer and more esoteric the words become, the more theological and philosophical is the jargon employed, and the more befuddled and bored the congregation becomes. Halford Luccock told of a preacher who, once a year, preached a sermon he knew was over the heads of his congregation—just so they would know he could do it! It was a cheap show of pride, as the apostle Paul realized so well when he took the Corinthian orators to task for their lofty words and worldly wisdom (I Cor. 1–2).

Of course, sometimes a preacher's words are unclear to a

congregation because the gospel is unclear to the preacher—the only thing such a preacher is able to do is repeat the theological jargon learned in seminary. There was once a student who could state all the theological theories of the atonement that he had learned from his textbooks, but he could not proclaim the message of the cross in simple and convincing pictures, because the message of the cross had never come home to his heart. The style is the man or woman!

In similar fashion, the language of the preacher should have *strength* and *energy*, employing strong nouns and active verbs in a vigorous delivery. Once I observed a minister who moved at a snail's pace about the chancel and who spoke in a tired and pious sigh, as if he were breathing his last. Yet the gospel he was called to preach is a Word of life—abundant, bubbling over, unconquerable, inexhaustable! That preacher's words and manner belied the fact that he had ever experienced it. The man and his inner deprivation were quite literally his style.

So too, a preacher's style should have *profundity*, dealing with the great issues of birth and life and death. No congregation will be deeply moved by themes and problems and questions that do not really matter. The temptation of a poor preacher is to try to move the people with sentimentality, to make them care by taking "cheap shots" at their emotions—covering them with bathos equivalent to love of gods and mothers and flags. But simple words—honest words which portray God and our relation to him; which talk about the meaning of the cares and sufferings we always know; which get at the guilt in our hopeless hearts and the anxiety in our frightened souls; which show how we often wound and hurt those we love most; which deal with the loss we know beside a grave or the joy we feel when we are accepted as we are; which talk about the helplessness of persons faced with overwhelming forces around them—simple words about these things get down to the nitty-gritty of our people's lives and deal with them in the profound terms with which God has dealt with them. But if preachers have not known God to deal with those things in their own lives, their preaching will not dip below the surface of sentimentality. The style is the woman or man.

Let it also be said that the style of every preacher should be *honest*.

Samuel Butler once spoke of the "irritating habit of theologians and preachers of telling little lies in the interest of a great truth."[3] We tend all too frequently to exaggeration in our preaching—of the immorality of groups we do not like, of simplistic differentiations between Christian and non-Christian living, of how easy it is to live out the gospel, of how effortlessly life's difficulties can be overcome. How often have scientists been attacked unfairly from the pulpit for their "atheism," or businessmen for their "materialism"! We have our whipping dogs that we use to arouse our congregations to righteous indignation, and then when aroused, they are reassured that it is quite simple to be good. Or we glibly proclaim an easy victory over their suffering. As James Stewart once put it, "I would implore you not to mock the bitterness of human hearts with facile phrases about the nobility of pain."[4] But we can be honest about those things only as we ourselves are one, in love, with our people, in the common, everyday struggle to live the gospel. Then we know honestly what that struggle involves. Our style from the pulpit is indeed our own manner of living.

The style of the preacher should also be *joyful*, which means that occasionally it will be marked with *humor*. If you think life is hopeless and your labor in vain, then there is very little you have to celebrate. But preachers who live in the Word know better, and their joy comes streaming forth in the words chosen and in the manner of their delivery. The style reflects the inner workings of the speaker.

Those who feel that joy in the Word cannot take themselves too seriously. As G. K. Chesterton once wrote, "Angels can fly because they take themselves so lightly." Those who know the joy of life in the Word, "fly" a little, inwardly; they do not see themselves as terribly important people, burdened down with the awesome task of giving life to the dead all by themselves, moving through the dismal reaches of a darkened and dying society which soon is going to sink to the lower reaches of hell. How can it? "God was in Christ reconciling the world to himself" (II Cor. 5:19), and that fact is cause for great merriment and feasting and laughter: We celebrate it at the banquet feast each time we sit down at the Lord's table. God laughs at our prides and presumptions, the psalmist tells us (Ps. 2), and so

God's people and we preachers have the ability to laugh at them too; that merriment bubbles out from the heart of the preacher who knows that God is in charge of the world and of his people sitting out there in the pews.

The preacher's style must always be *appropriate*, however. The context of preaching is worship, and we do not behave flippantly before the living God, nor do we tell jokes that have nothing to do with his reign. Some preachers wish to be funny in the pulpit just to call attention to their own sense of humor. I knew one student who gave the impression of being more stand-up comedian than pastor. Humor spills out from the pulpit because God has put all things in proper perspective—our pompousness, our defeats, our sufferings, our deaths. But if we do not know about that work of God in our lives, our humor in the pulpit becomes a sad joke, told by idiots, signifying nothing. The style truly is a reflection of the experience of the preacher.

The preacher's style is simple and honest, humble, and accompanied sometimes with laughter, but it also is filled with overwhelming *conviction*. Let us never mistake doubt in the pulpit for humility. Sometimes preachers are so worried about taking notice of every point of view and so fearful of imposing their own thoughts on their people, that they preach a gospel framed in the terms of "it may be." Once in a seminar with Karl Barth, a student ended a paper with the statement, "Perhaps Christ is coming again." "Not 'perhaps'!" Barth roared. "Say it! Christ is coming again!" We know. We know whom we have believed, and there is no doubt about his victory. Only if our style conveys that certainty can our people have any hope at all. Our message is not "It may be that Jesus Christ is risen." Our Good News always and everywhere is, "Jesus Christ is risen Lord!" No ifs, ands, or buts!—not if we know him risen in our own hearts and lives! Our style is the mirror of our own conviction.

Finally, the style of the preacher should always have *beauty and eloquence*. By that I do not mean that our language should not be that of everyday simplicity. But there is a euphony about the English language when it is properly used. Consider the following from the end of an ecological sermon on "God the Music Lover," based on Psalm 148 and Colossians 1:9-20.

> Our scripture lesson from Colossians proclaims that all things hold together in Christ. And perhaps this is finally the way we affirm that is really true—by so loving our God in his Son that we will not disrupt the song of one old man or child; that we will not still a single sparrow's song raised to him in praise, or pollute the waters of one fish that bubbles out its joy, or condone the setting out of a trap of poison for one coyote howling his hallelujah. Then indeed God's universe can be joined together as one, sounding forth its great, unbroken Te Deum in one united chorus of praise, for the love that God has lavished upon us in his Son. And God the music lover can hear and smile and rejoice over his work and affirm once again, as he did at the beginning, "Behold, it is very good."[5]

There are no big words in that paragraph, but it contains rhythm and alliteration and onomatopoeia. The phrasing was not calculated, however; it flowed automatically, as the writer was caught up in the universal song of praise of the psalm.

If we will only realize that we have to do with a God of incomparable glory and majesty, we will not feel so inhibited about the language we use to describe him. It can soar and sing and stretch our imaginative talents to their limits, and still it is not adequate to express his love for us in Jesus Christ. Paul always felt God's love had no boundaries: "Neither death, nor life, nor angels, nor principalities, nor things present, nor things to come, nor powers, nor height, nor depth, nor anything else in all creation . . ." His disciple in Ephesians took up the song and spoke of Christ's "unsearchable riches" and prayed that we might know "the breadth and length and height and depth" of the love of Christ "which surpasses knowledge." When we preachers know that love of God for us in his Son, our words flow in some semblance of eloquence and harmony. But there is no way to inspire such language other than to know fully, day by day, the One of whom we speak. The style is the man or woman, in love with God, because God has first loved us. Our language mirrors the engagement of our hearts.

SPEAKING IN PICTURES

Having said all that, now let me add some qualifications. I have implied that style is automatic—that it is more a matter of faith and life than of craft and deliberation. And yet there are some technical ways to improve our style, which will supplement the disciplines already mentioned in chapter 2.

In the first place, we can learn from the Bible's concreteness. There is no book with language more specific. For examples, read Jeremiah's portrayal of a drought throughout the land of Judah in 14:2-6 or study the scathing description of a dying King David in II Kings 1:1-4. The Bible's language gets right down to cases.

I wrote an article for a denominational journal a number of years ago, in which I spoke of "Job, covered with sores." The editor of the journal preferred not to be that specific. He changed the phrase to "Job, confronted with seemingly insurmountable difficulties." But the Bible does not hedge in its language about us and about our sins. Read Isaiah 1:2-6 for an example.

I think the Bible talks that way because God's language is so specific: "And the Lord said to Isaiah, 'Go forth to meet Ahaz, you and Shearjashub your son, at the end of the conduit of the upper pool on the highway to the Fuller's Field' " (Isa. 7:3). We have a God who is so particular in his speaking that he gives his prophet highway directions!

The Bible's God always gets down to cases. He does not tell us to love all people; he commands us to love our neighbor, because our neighbor is a very specific person, right there on the spot. He does not ask us to show mercy in general; he points to the thirsty, the hungry, the imprisoned, the naked, and questions whether we have ministered to their very particular needs. He does not reveal himself everywhere and always; he says, "This is my beloved Son . . . Listen to him." He does not ask for a general consensus of opinion about that Son; Jesus' question is, "But who do you say that I am?" Descriptions, commands, actions, decisions—these all have to do with specifics in the Bible, and if we would preach its Good News, we also must learn to be that specific.

It is not that, from the pulpit, we single out certain persons in our congregations—we must never do so; or that we talk about individual problems, revealing counseling confidences—that is something a preacher does not do, ever! Rather, the language we use in our sermons is concrete language, which always gets down to cases. For example, we do not talk about forgiveness in general; we speak of the willingness of a wife to forget her husband has been unfaithful, or the new beginning given a parent when a child, after being unjustly punished, hugs her and says, "I love you, Mommy."

Our words themselves are concrete nouns and verbs. On this score, we can take a lesson from the psalmists. Psalm 104 speaks of trees, but these quickly become the cedars and the firs. There is mention of beasts, but the picture switches to wild asses and grazing cattle. The psalmist speaks of the birds of the air, but then talks about the stork. The general always becomes specific; the abstract is always concretized. In Psalm 103, the singer begins with the call to his soul to "forget not all [the Lord's] benefits," but then those benefits are, one by one, spelled out: the forgiveness of wrong, the healing of diseases, the buying back from death, the renewal of vitality. When we speak of the blessings of the Lord on our congregation, let us enumerate those blessings with concrete nouns and verbs.

The specific words of the Bible cannot be separated from the pictures those words draw, and everywhere, we can learn from the Bible's imagery. The forgiveness mentioned in Psalm 103 quickly turns into pictures:

> For as the heavens are high above the earth,
>   so great is his steadfast love toward those who fear him;
> as far as the east is from the west,
>   so far does he remove our transgressions from us.
> As a father pities his children,
>   so the Lord pities those who fear him.
> For he knows our frame;
>   he remembers that we are dust.
> As for man, his days are like grass;
>   he flourishes like a flower of the field;
> for the wind passes over it, and it is gone,
>   and its place knows it no more.

Such pictures are found on almost every page of the Scriptures, and it is in such pictorial language that we preachers must finally learn to speak, in order that our people can see new images in the imaginations of their hearts. The question is, How do we learn to do that?

We do so by constantly using similes and metaphors. You will notice that several of the lines in the preceding psalm begin with "as," while the next lines start with "so"; that is a simile. God's forgiveness is compared to something else—here, to the immensities of space. Then there is a comparison of man to grass and to the flower of the field; that is a metaphor—a longer comparison between two things. Similes and metaphors enlarge our vision and understanding and allow us to experience a new world by speaking of the unknown in terms of the known.

Suppose we ask, Who is God? We do not know who he is in himself, but from the Bible's similes and metaphors, we do know that in relation to his people he is like a shepherd, a father, a husband, a king, a lover, a bridegroom, a warrior, a master, a vineyard owner, a lord, a consuming fire, a redeemer of a slave, a savior, a never-failing stream, a rock, a fortress, a lion, a bear robbed of her cubs, a moth, a fountain of living water, a way, a light, bread from heaven, a shield, a potter, a mother, a sword-wielder, an ax-wielder, a judge, a plaintiff, a witness in a court—the list can be extended almost indefinitely. These are the similes and metaphors by which the Bible lets us experience the reality of God. They describe him by images with which we are already familiar, and through them we begin to know who God is.

Or let us ask, What is sin? In the language of the Bible, sin is like becoming a harlot when one is married, or rebelling against a father's love and leaving home, or attempting to storm heaven, or forgetting the past, or wandering away like a sheep, or becoming a subversive in a nation, or not being dressed when one is supposed to be ready for a wedding, or becoming like a rotten bunch of grapes in a well-tended vineyard, or trying to drink from an empty cistern when an ever-flowing stream is nearby, or breaking into a house by stealth, or leaning against a feeble reed, or thinking one is divorced when one is really married, or making empty promises, or failing to release a neighbor from a debt, or grumbling over a neighbor's good fortune, or being blind, or being imprisoned, or being enslaved, or never being born, or being lame, or being deaf, or missing a path, or not knowing what time it is, or distorting the laws of nature, or being like a bird in a snare or a prey for wild beasts. The figures almost shout out the foolishness of our ways, and through such similes and metaphors we begin to have a sense of our helplessness and rebellion and idiocy.

We speak in terms of what we know, to illumine what we do not know. Thus the Bible itself guides us in understanding its message, and we should copy that style of speech in our sermons.

In using similes and metaphors, we should make them as varied as the Bible's; we should use pictures from modern life as often as possible—though many of the Bible's images remain vivid for our age; and we should appeal to all the senses in the pictures we use. Consider this excerpt from a Thanksgiving meditation, given during a period of widespread third-world famine.

> Imagine for yourself for one minute the sounds that will rise up to God next Thursday afternoon. He will hear our mumbled prayers of thanksgiving for our juicy turkey, and he will hear the crying of an Asian baby, whose skeleton shows through its skin. God will hear the pounding of football cleats from hundreds of stadiums around the United States, and he will hear the scraping of the hands of African women as they sift through the dust of the ground for any overlooked grain of wheat. The Lord will hear the crack of a number-two wood hitting a golf ball from the well-fertilized tees of countless golf courses, and he will hear the voice of a Congo farmer, begging for fertilizer for his crops. And somehow I do not believe that our God will be pleased with what he hears.[6]

The metaphor is of God the listener; the images are those that appeal to ear and eye, in order that the congregation may see and hear along with God and may identify with his attitude toward his world.

One of the greatest masters of sense appeal was Charles Haddon Spurgeon, and while many of his figures are now out-of-date, look how he used them:

(the sense of sound) Our hearts like muffled drums, are beating funeral marches to the tomb.

(the sense of touch) The heart is very slippery. Yes. The heart is a fish that troubles all gospel fishermen to hold . . . slimy as an eel, it slippeth between your fingers.

(the sense of taste) Suppose you tell me that honey is bitter. I reply, "No, I am sure you cannot have tasted it; taste it and try." So it is with the Holy Ghost.

(the sense of smell) The precious perfume of the gospel must be poured forth to sweeten the air.[7]

There are also these phrases in the sermon by James Stewart:

(the senses of touch and smell) You are not prisoners behind the bars of a narrow earthbound existence, where men push and jostle one another for their tawdry, perishable prizes, and breathe the suffocating, poisonous air of a materialist philosophy.

(the sense of sight) This highway of the spirit tends to get blocked by the dust and drudgery of life.

(the sense of sound) For when our sins cry out to God for punishment and vengeance, something else also happens . . . the blood of Christ cries louder, overbears and drowns and silences the very crying of our sins, and God for Christ's sake forgives.[8]

Metaphors and similes that appeal to all the senses enlist the whole listener in response to the gospel, as he sees it, touches it, tastes it, smells it, and hears it in his imagination.

We must be careful when using metaphors, however, not to use too many and not to mix them so that the minds of the people are filled with a jumble of images. Rather, the picture we sketch out in their imaginations by our language must be single and clear, in order that they may experience it. If we introduce conflicting pictures, the whole loses its power. Do not begin by talking about shepherds and wolves and later on talk about fishermen and hurricanes, or the congregation will probably think about Sunday afternoon football and rival quarterbacks.

Despite the cautions given in chapter 2 about using biblical language, it is also true that many of the biblical motifs are so powerful and are embedded so pervasively in the biblical story that they retain a force which still can be put to very good use today. For example, the motif of primeval chaos runs throughout the Bible, from the first chapter of Genesis to the last of Revelation—that dark, lifeless, shadowy nothingness of death; that stormy, watery, evil void, empty of all order and light; that primal disorder from which other peoples said their gods had emanated. It is a figure reflected in so much of our life today—in the apocalyptic mushroom clouds of our atomic explosions; in the desolating barrenness that chokes a heart when a divorce is final. One day I drove behind a young girl in a sports car, with a bumper sticker bearing only one word—CHAOS; perhaps it was her perception of the nature of her society. Our people know what chaos is; they live with it every day, and they desperately need the glad announcement that God is sovereign over it. Thus the way the figure is used and the biblical witness to God's victory over chaos are symbols still very pertinent to our preaching.

The same is true of many of the figures of the Bible: the stories and sayings about fathers and sons, or about mothers weeping for their children; the figures of light and sunrise and dawn; the symbols of warfare and suffering and struggle; the security symbols—refuge, fortress, hiding place, the "mighty rock within a weary land." Such expressions, and many others too numerous to mention, touch our universal human condition and can be put to good use in modern preaching.

One of the most effective ways to use the Bible's pictures is to pair the use of a picture in the Old Testament with a similar one in the New. There is a scene in a garden in Genesis, and also in the passion story. There are wilderness temptations in both Testaments. In the Old Testament, there is a disobedient son; in the New, an obedient one. There are old covenant and new, rotten vine and true vine, unfaithful shepherds and good shepherd, unrighteous kings and righteous king, old commandments and new, first exodus and second. Both Testaments speak of a yoke, a cup, a way, a stone of stumbling, a cornerstone, a temple, a pilgrimage, light, and living water. Both have a passover, an atonement, a mercy seat, a camp, a Melchizedek, a Mosaic prophet, a suffering servant. There is a healing figure lifted up in both old and new covenants; there is, in both, a feeding of a multitude, a raising of the dead, an Elijah. The list can be expanded almost endlessly. These are traditional motifs and personages—symbols used to carry the sacred story—and all of them bear pictures. We can use those pictures as they have been used through two thousand years of Christian preaching—to let our people see and feel and enter into the sacred story.

If we can do that through our language, by polishing and honing it until it can be used by God as the two-edged sword of his Word, then perhaps our people will begin to see that their lives have a glory about them—that they are not simply living out a daily grind from 9:00 to 5:00; that they are not just involved in the day-to-day repetition of cleaning and washing and cooking; that their days are not to be "measured out in coffee spoons" at home or in production figures at the office. No, perhaps then our people will begin to see that there is a great cosmic drama going on—one in which we all are players—and that each of us is called to add to the story until it is completed. If we live into the Bible's story, it is "center stage" for all of us. First Abraham and Moses and the psalmists and the white-robed company of martyrs played their roles; Amos and Isaiah and the goodly fellowship of the prophets; then Paul and John, Augustine and Anselm, Luther and Calvin and Knox, Damien and Bonhoeffer and King, and finally you and I and Mrs. Jones. We all are called to play the Christian before our sovereign—to *become* the part, to add the next sentence to the drama—while God from the throne, and his Son, and all the ministering spirits watch breathlessly to hear each line and to mark each movement, and the whole universe waits and waits in hope for the final triumphant curtain.

There is an eternal drama at stake in and through and behind our ordinary lives, and by the use of holy imagination, we preachers are called to awaken our people to the part we, separately and together, play in it. To let our words become the vehicle of God's continuing drive toward his kingdom, his rule over all the earth—that is the goal and measure of all our creativity.

VII. THE USE AND ABUSE OF ILLUSTRATIONS

An illustration is, by definition, that which illumines a topic. As Jowett somewhere wrote, "The best illustrations should be like honest street lamps, scarcely noticed, but throwing floods of light upon the road." The metaphors and similes and pictorial language that were discussed in the last chapter could, in this sense, be classed as illustrations, and some preachers' language is so full of these that their sermons need no other illustrative material. The congregation is continually treated to mental images by the very nature of the speech. For example, further illustrations added to the pictures drawn in the sermon by Peter Marshall would only have been intrusive. [1]

However, most of us preach thematic and proclamational sermons, whose major portions are made up of affirmations and ideas and arguments, and we need to intersperse the thought portions with picture portions, in order to make our speech vivid and concrete and clear. We need illustrations in our sermons because we do not talk constantly in pictures. Illustrations are, for ordinary preachers, our substitutes for not being poets.

LEGITIMATE AND ILLEGITIMATE USES

The use of illustrations in itself can be a fine art, and the abuse of that art has ruined many sermons. The purpose of illustrations is strictly utilitarian: They are to make clear that which is being said—to make it concrete; to bring it down to cases, so that our people may identify with it and say, "Yes, that is my life and story." But there are preachers who construct entire sermons of nothing but illustrations, and for some reason, that is one traditional method of preaching in Methodism. I have heard dozens of Methodist preachers who do nothing more than preach what D. M. Lloyd-Jones has called "skyscraper sermons"—one story on top of another.[2] Sometimes little moral lessons are drawn from the stories as they are told, but essentially, illustrative material is the sole content of the sermon. Gerald Kennedy's sermon teeters on the edge of this fault, although he does include more solid content than do many of his brethren.[3]

Again, there are preachers who use illustrations simply as ornamentations. The illustrations add nothing to the comprehensibility of the sermon; rather, they burden it down and bring its movement to a screeching halt while the preacher tells a story, and sometimes the congregation feels that the point being made is so obvious that the preacher is beating it to death with overemphasis. "That's a cute story, preacher," may be the congregational reaction, "but let's get on with the sermon"; or more devastating still, "That's a humorous performance, Reverend, but what does it have to do with God?"

There are also preachers, unfortunately, who use illustrations to show off their own erudition or status. The principal stumbling block for all clergy is our own pride, and some translate that into the illustrative material they foist off on their people: quotations from great thinkers (though usually looked up in Bartlett's); fine points of Hebrew and Greek etymology or extraneous details from the commentaries; recountings of wide travels through Christendom (a characteristic of some jetting church executives); or esoteric information about the preacher's speciality or hobby. No one in the congregation identifies with such information, because it is not designed to serve that purpose; its purpose is just the opposite—to set apart the preacher as someone special. And so in our pride, we preach ourselves and not Jesus Christ as Lord.

In other words, illustrating can be overdone and even sinfully done, and we have to be very careful how we use it. As in our previous discussion of experimental sermon forms, the question to ask of an illustration, also, is, Does this enable the congregation to identify with the biblical story? Good illustrations may grab a congregation at the beginning of a sermon by showing them that the text is about their lives, and then more illustrations may sustain that interest throughout the entire length of the delivery by making every point crystal clear and by forming pictures of its concrete meaning in the people's minds. Good illustrations, by personalizing the biblical message, may drive it home to some reluctant heart. Or good illustrations, which catch the mood of the congregational response to the Word, may give voice to the faith the sermon has aroused and verbalize the people's "Yes, yes. Oh yes!"

Illustrations also may serve a function in the structuring of the sermon. If they are well placed, they can add to the variety of pace in the sermon. Let us suppose you are moving along with the thought in narrative fashion. Then you pause with an illustration, repeating the thought in a picture or in different words. The narrative content is thereby given concreteness, the congregation has the opportunity to live into it more fully, and they have a break in which they may pause and reflect before you move them on.

Two cautions must be added. First, do not let the congregation get bogged down in any illustration; keep them moving forward. This means that all illustrations should be rather short. There are some preachers who tell stories, or recount scenes from movies or plays, or quote passages that are much too long. The result is that the sermon's drive toward its climax is interrupted, the congregation forgets what is being illustrated—that is, they forget the main point you wanted to make—and they usually remember nothing from the sermon except the illustration. If you want to preach a parabolic or allegorical or narrative sermon, made up entirely of some story, do so. But do not ruin other sermon forms by letting the illustrative material dominate.

Second, if the illustration is longer than a line or two, do not use two such illustrations back to back. Save the second anecdote or quote or picture for another sermon. Heaven knows you will need all the illustrative material you can find, and you do not need to load it all into one presentation. An illustration that immediately follows another, once again, halts the forward movement of the sermon. It also runs the risk of forming a competing image in the minds of the congregation, and the jumble results in the loss of the effects of both illustrations.

Occasionally an illustration can be used to move the thought of the sermon forward—that is, a paragraph in your manuscript can begin with an illustration which advances the sermon's thought and deals with content not dealt with previously. But the thought carried by the illustration must be very clear, and you should then expound on it. Never let illustrations alone carry the thought of a sermon. As George Buttrick used to tell his homiletics students, "Put it in your own fine words." We speak out of our faith to our people's faith, and no illustration can substitute for that personal address.

If we do nothing else, we should tell the truth, and that means that in using illustrations, we must not forget the facts. Preachers are tempted sometimes to embroider stories in order to make them more useful in the pulpit. Sometimes we recount incidents which happened to other people as if they had happened to us. Such tamperings with truth never ring quite true; they undermine our own growth in sanctification, and thus they finally undermine our witness to the gospel. There is enough illustrative material available to us without the necessity of perjuring ourselves.

Our illustrations should be quite varied in nature. We may have a hobby, but we should not always use it as our source of illustrative material; many in the congregation may have no interest in our interest at all. Rather, with Paul, in our use of illustrations, we should try to "become all things to all men, that [we] might by all means save some" (I Cor. 9:22). We should use illustrations for all the sorts and conditions of our people, touching on the varied aspects and interests of their individual lives. Here is an excerpt from an Eastertide sermon, preached to an affluent congregation.

You and I are rather superficial people at times. We worried about how our new clothes looked when we dressed for church this morning. We are unhappy that we bought that latest block of stock at 23¼, when, if we had been on our toes, we could have gotten it at 23. We nag at the kids because the courses they are following at school are not sufficiently feeding our parental pride. But here, now, in this Eastertide, we are concerned with life and death.[4]

Several different groups were appealed to, in three very brief pictures and, incidentally, when the block of stock was mentioned, the head of every businssman in the congregation came up.

We must be very careful about our facts, however. If we are using an illustration from economics or medicine or natural science or some other equivalent body of knowledge, we will undermine our sermon's effectiveness if we have our facts wrong. Nothing disturbs professionals or scholars or practitioners in some field quite so much as to have a preacher distort the facts from that field of knowledge. Their conclusion is that the preacher does not know what he or she is talking about, and thus the gospel as a whole is discredited. Especially has this been true in relation to American business practices. Many preachers have not the foggiest notion of economics or of how the American marketplace works. Yet the materialism and economic greed of society are favorite targets for criticism from the pulpit. The criticism would be much more responsively received if representatives of both management and labor in our congregations were convinced that preachers understand money matters. So it is, too, with other fields of knowledge. We must know our facts before we use them in sermon illustrations.

Finally, no illustration should need to be explained. Either it should illumine immediately, or it should not be used. So too, no incident or scene from a movie or book or similar source should be employed if it is necessary to go to great lengths to explain its context. It must be of illustrative import in itself. We can never assume that all our listeners have read a particular book or seen a particular movie or play or TV program, no matter how popular such may be. Thus we also cannot assume that our people know an excerpt's original context. We are limited to using those incidents and scenes that are clear in themselves or that need only a phrase or two to explain their characters and setting. If an illustration interrupts the forward flow of a sermon for more than a moment or two, then it probably is an illustration that should not be used.

SOURCES AND TYPES OF ILLUSTRATIONS

The field for gathering illustrative material is as broad as human life itself. There is no corner from which we may not collect an anecdote, an observation, a striking saying. Pictures leap out at us on every hand, to give concreteness to the gospel, to portray the nature of human life, to set the Word of God into juxtaposition with human beings. What better sources are there for finding portrayals of the social situation of our congregation than the daily newspapers, magazines, telecasts, and advertisements? These mirror our motives and minds every day, often in brief and striking images.

At the same time, our constant reading of classics and poetry, history and drama, biography and fiction, furnishes us with new insights and language and pictures with which we may portray God's relation to us and ours to him. Look at just one excerpt from Hardy's *Tess of the D'Urbervilles.*

> "Did you say the stars were worlds, Tess?"
> "Yes."
> "All like ours?"
> "I don't know; but I think so. They sometimes seem to be like apples on our stubbard tree. Most of them splendid and sound—a few blighted."
> "Which do we live on—a splendid one or a blighted one?"
> "A blighted one."

Such pictures may be found almost inexhaustively in our reading.

Imaginative observations of the natural world are a constant source of illustrations, just as are reflections on the findings of medicine and geology and physics. Biography, history, travel, athletics, art, psychology, anthropology—no field of human endeavor is without its illustrations of the works of human beings or its analogies to the works of God. After all, it is God and we who are involved in every enterprise.

The art of illustration is constantly to see the world around us in the light of the Word of God, and to carry on that running inner dialogue of which I have spoken, between the biblical revelation and human life. For instance, I have been reading accounts showing why scientists may have thought life came out of the primal ooze in the abyss of the sea. Now we know better; human life had need of light and air and green—and thus I have an illustration for a sermon on Genesis 1. The songs of humpback whales, recorded by scientists, furnished an illustration for a sermon on Psalm 148. An alcoholic friend's travail was a picture of our captivity in the sermon from Deuteronomy, outlined in chapter 4.

Everything around the preacher speaks back to him or her in relation to the Word of God. For example, a new opera entitled *Paradise Lost* was recently performed at Lincoln Center; six male voices sang the role of the voice of God. The reviews reported that the opera was a flop. Surely this might illustrate the fact that we do not replace God very well! Even the junk mail that comes across our desks bears its significance. Last year I received an advertising brochure from a religious publishing house, offering all sorts of printed and audio-visual materials to aid pastors in their work. On the front, it read, "Relax, Pastor! Your Lent/Easter planning just became easier with"—and then on the inside, in large letters— "the Trials of Jesus Program!" What a commentary on our attitudes toward the cross! Or read the ads for jeweled crosses in *The New Yorker*—"Your friends will admire your excellent taste," the advertisers tell us. Everything in human life comments on our relationship to God because everything in human life is involved in that relationship. We preachers simply have to be alert enough, knowing the Word through and through, to see and hear the examples that focus the commentary into one telling scene or sentence.

Also not to be ignored as a source for illustrative material is the rich history of the church. We have two thousand years of that history of human wrestling and faith and experience with the Word of God. The lives of saints and martyrs and ordinary Christians; the distillation of a period's faith in its particular creed; stories from the mission field; hymns and sermons and doctrinal statements—these all are replete with reflections on the action of God in human life and are sources of countless pictures and creative portrayals.

Finally, there are the illustrative materials of the Bible itself: the experiences of Israel and of the early church; the testimonies of thousands of voices—in laments and hymns, thanksgivings and prayers, creeds and proverbs, liturgies and enthronement songs—all mirror human life in relation to our God, and they can be used to show us our life in relation to him also.

As there are many different sources of illustrative material, so there are all types of illustrations. In addition to those already mentioned, there are also brief anecdotes—incidents with real characters. Here is one used by George Buttrick:

> A man was fishing one day when a shepherd came by looking for some sheep that were lost. "How did you lose them?" asked the fisherman. "Oh, they just nibble their way lost and can't find the way back again."

There are historical or biographical allusions:

> Henrik Ibsen, age 60, in a letter to an 18-year-old flirt, with whom he had become infatuated: "You and the Christmas season do not quite fit together."

There are brief quotations from the news media, such as this from a *Newsweek* interview with pop singer John Denver:

> I reflect in a very real way where humanity is . . . where we're going. . . . I can do anything. One of these days I'll be so complete I won't be human. I'll be a god.[5]

There are short parables and allegories. Here is one from James Stewart:

Faust, in the old story, gambled with his soul: and an artist has painted a picture—a game of chess, Faust at one side, Satan at the other. The game in the picture is almost over, and Faust has only a few pieces left, a king, a knight, one or two pawns; and on his face there is a look of blank despair, while at the other side of the board the devil leers in anticipation of his coming triumph. Many a chess-player has looked at the picture and agreed that the position is hopeless; it is checkmate. But one day in the picture-gallery a great master of the game stood gazing at the picture. He was fascinated by the look of terrible despair on the face of Faust. Then his gaze went to the pieces on the board. He stared at them absorbed. Other visitors in the gallery came and went, and still he studied the board, lost in contemplation. And then suddenly the gallery was startled by a ringing shout: "It is a lie! The king and the knight have another move!" . . . THE KING AND THE KNIGHT HAVE ANOTHER MOVE.[6]

Occasionally we use illustrative incidents from our own personal experience, but these must be employed infrequently and with great restraint. We are tempted to tell our congregations all the clever things our children say or all the marvelous personal insights we gain about our own inner workings, but we should resist such temptations with all self-discipline, in order not to put ourselves or our families at the center of our message.

The question sometimes arises, What types of illustrations are inadmissable in the pulpit? Certainly any stories that bear racial or religious slurs, or that are delivered in the dialect of a particular people, have no place in the one body of Christ. Illustrations that partake of sensationalism and gossip, or that even border on the prurient and titilating are unworthy vehicles of the gospel of the love of God. So too are passages that grow out of the preacher's own economic or political prejudices and that have no relation to the biblical text.

There are also times when a preacher must consider very carefully whether to mention an event that has been on the front pages of the newspaper. Human life can be shocking and raw and sometimes so immersed in degradation that it is difficult to imagine human beings who would descend to the depths reported. Cases of child abuse, sexual murders of adolescents, drug orgies, deliberate torching of human beings, victims stalked on city streets or clubbed to death for a thrill—these horrors are part and parcel of American society—just as are mate-swappings and rapes in schools and alcoholism in the halls of Congress. The preacher has to decide with what events to deal and how realistically to portray them. On the one hand, there is no religion that looks evil so steadily in the face as does the Christian faith with its bloody cross. Human life on its ugliest level is portrayed in the Bible and met by God in Christ, head on, to be redeemed and purified. If that is the sermon's aim—to redeem human life, to let God work his transforming will upon it or through his alerted people—then let the preacher use the illustrations necessary for that purpose. But if the aim is only to be sensational or judgmental, or even to frighten the congregation into faith, then the preacher should reevaluate his or her goals and find better illustrative material. If we cling fast to the purpose of our preaching—to mediate the action of God—then more often than not, our efforts will be appropriate and seemly and fitting to the setting of worship.

At the other extreme, the preacher should be careful to avoid all sentimentalism. This is probably the most frequent error in the use of illustrations—substituting for the gospel of God the sentiments of gush. We tell tear-prompting stories about children or animals, and the women open their purses to find their hankies. We quote awful poetry or idealize some sinful human being. We surround Jesus with sweetness and light, especially at Christmastime. We turn God into a kindly, forgiving old grandfather, or we find him only in peace and beauty. Then we wonder why our preaching makes no difference in our people's lives and why their lives make no changes in the society around them. The answer is of course that such preaching is not dealing with God or human life as they actually are. The gospel has been turned into a lovely tale from Never-Never Land, having nothing to do with the suffering, the decisions, the ambiguities, the struggles of life in American society. I sometimes think the best compliment we can receive after a sermon is to have someone press our hand and say, "You told it like it is."

On this score, we especially need to be careful about the poetry we use in sermons. In the first place, we rarely should include more than two or three lines of poetry in any sermon. If it is good poetry, our people probably will not be able to follow the meaning of more than that, because they hear it only once. Bad poetry is easier to follow, but it trivializes the gospel. If you have no literary training, then use only passages from the recognized poets. They have won their place in great literature with their images and use of language, their rhythm and profundity of thought. Surely, God should be honored with nothing less.

If we quote hymns in our sermons, again, we should try to use the best. There are trivial and sentimental hymns, just as there are trivial and sentimental poems, but there are also some magnificent hymnic expressions of faith. These can be used to witness to the congregation or to express the people's silent thoughts and feelings. We should not, however, get into the habit of ending every sermon with a quotation from a hymn. And as with poetry, it is best to use only two or three lines. Brevity, rather than length, is always a good rule to follow in using any illustrative material.

COLLECTING AND STORING ILLUSTRATIVE MATERIAL

We should eschew the use of all books of sermon illustrations. Often their material is hackneyed or out-of-date, or if it does have merit, the congregation may have heard some of it before. Above all, the illustrations in such collections have not passed through the loom of your experience—have not been woven into the fabric of your meeting with the Word of God on behalf of your people. Good illustrations encapsulate, in vivid image or striking expression or elucidating contrast, your meeting with the biblical Word in company with your congregation. Nothing substitutes for that personal and priestly meeting, and your illustrations should be your own reflections of it and on it.

We do, occasionally, borrow illustrative material from other preachers. We do, and should, read and study others' sermons and methods, and profit from others' faith. They are part of the company of saints out of whose faith we speak and by whose witness we are sustained. But if we do borrow illustrations, we should acknowledge their source, to let our congregations realize that we are speaking out of the faith of the church and not simply out of our own experience. Then our people, too, may be strengthened and sustained by the communion of saints. And once again, any borrowed material must pass through our own priestly meeting with the Word of God in order to be a true expression of that lively meeting.

Certainly it is best to collect our own illustrations. In our running dialogue with the Word of God as it meets human life, we should constantly be jotting down and storing up images, pictures, sayings, quotations, poetry, anecdotes, and analogies which will help us express that meeting. We cannot rely on memory to store up such material; the Word speaks in some instant *kairos*, and it is very difficult to recapture it unless we have recorded it in one form or another. Even all the kairoi of the Bible had finally to be written down, to preserve them for the generations that came after.

The form we choose for collecting and storing illustrations is largely up to each of us. Some preachers keep elaborate file-card systems. Some have loose-leaf notebooks, classified according to subject. Some simply drop jottings and musings into a shoe box and then go through them occasionally, although the lack of any classification system usually means the illustrations will never be used, because they are too difficult to locate in the pressure of preparing a sermon. On the other hand, no classification system ever quite fits, and we file an illustration under one subject, only to find that it applies to another when we come to the actual task of sermon writing. The main thing is to have the material as available as possible, and each of us has to devise his or her own system for achieving that.

Once or twice a year we should go through the material and cull that which has become out-of-date. Many illustrations quickly lose their relevance and cutting edge; the times change and the Word of God is constantly saying new things in new situations. If we do not cull, the file or notebook becomes so large as to be almost unmanageable—that is, it does if we are carrying on a constant dialogue with the Word. Those ministers who live with the Word of God burning in their bones hear, on every hand, so many illustrations pertinent to that Word that their collections never lack for new additions. How constant is God's activity and speech in relation to human life!

The ideal, of course, is to plan one's preaching so that one knows in advance the texts one will be using for several weeks or months. This is one of the enormous advantages of preaching from a lectionary. Thus in all the moments of leisure, of waiting, of driving from meeting to meeting, a text can be mulled over and allowed to work in the mind and heart, while at the same time illustrations appropriate to that particular text present themselves in one's reading and experiences and can be stored up with that particular sermon in mind. Indeed, the illustrative material—the way the Word meets with human life—helps shape the sermon as a whole, and we are enabled to speak out of the meeting point of the Word and the congregational situation.

On the other hand, we should not store up only those illustrations pertinent to a sermon or text already planned. Any incident or picture or saying that enters into the dialogue with the Word of God may, even ten years later, find its appropriate place in a sermon. Some illustrative material never grows antiquated, because it speaks of the universal human condition, or it profoundly witnesses to the working of God yesterday, today, and forever. That is material to be treasured and stored and used when the time is fulfilled.

In collecting illustrative material, we also sometimes find a quotation or poem or incident apparently so illuminating of the Word of God that the illustration itself prompts the formation of a sermon around it. This is dangerous. It can be a legitimate practice if the illustrative material points vividly to a text and sets us working with the Word, so that the sermon finally grows out of the text and not out of the illustration. But the danger is that the illustrative material will impose a meaning on the text which is not properly there and therefore may lead us to ignore the text in order to preserve the use of the illustration. Only if the text, as it is carefully exegeted, and the illustration join together as common mediators of the Word of God to a particular situation, can an illustration be allowed to exercise such a prominent part in the construction of the sermon. We are called to preach the Word of God. We are expected by God and by the congregation alike to be faithful to that calling.

In looking back over the course we have covered in this volume, I cannot help but have the feeling of incompleteness. How can one fully convey what it means to preach creatively? There are Christian disciplines, homiletical principles, methods of exegesis and style, which one can attempt to explain to students of homiletics. But all the way along I have known that that is not sufficient. Creative preaching finally happens only when God in Christ lays hold of our lives and works his transforming new creation in heart and mind and action. Then words catch fire, and love is born, and the Christian community becomes reality; and God presses forward toward the goal of his kingdom on earth. I only know that God does so act, if we are faithful to him. If we will work—if we will dedicate ourselves to his service in study and discipline and devotion and obedience—he will enlist us as participants in the miracle of saving his beloved people. "It has pleased God through the folly of the message we preach to save those who believe." I know of no higher purpose for our work and talents and lives.

NOTES

CHAPTER I: CREATIVITY AND AUTHORITY

1. Robert Frost, "To Earthward," from *The Poetry of Robert Frost*, edited by Edward Connery Lathem. Copyright 1923, © 1969 by Holt, Rinehart & Winston. Copyright 1951 by Robert Frost. Reprinted by permission of Holt, Rinehart & Winston, Publishers. British rights granted by Jonathan Cape Limited on behalf of the Estate of Robert Frost.
2. W. H. Auden, "For the Time Being."
3. From Handel's *Messiah*.

CHAPTER II: THE NATURE AND DEVELOPMENT OF CREATIVITY

1. Helen Keller, *The Story of My Life* (Garden City, N.Y.: Doubleday & Company, 1954), pp. 36, 34.
2. *Newsweek*, June 25, 1979, p. 84.
3. William Ernest Henley, "Invictus," from *Echoes*.
4. Richard W. Weaver, *Language Is Sermonic: Richard M. Weaver on the Nature of Rhetoric*, ed. R. L. Johannsen, R. Strickland, and R. T. Eubanks (Baton Rouge: Louisiana State University Press, 1970), p. 30.
5. October 15, 1956.
6. Strunk and White, *Elements of Style*, 2d ed. (New York: The Macmillan Company, 1972); Newman, *Strictly Speaking* (New York: Warner Press, 1975).
7. William Faulkner, from his acceptance speech upon receiving the Nobel prize for literature.
8. Jay E. Adams, *Sense Appeal in the Sermons of Charles Haddon Spurgeon* (Grand Rapids: Baker Book House, 1975), p. 5.
9. Gerard Manley Hopkins, "God's Grandeur," *Poems and Prose of Gerard Manley Hopkins*, ed. W. H. Gardner (New York: Penguin Books, 1978), p. 27.
10. Rudolph Bohren, *Preaching and Community*, trans. David E. Green (Richmond: John Knox Press, 1965), p. 63.

11. Reinhold Niebuhr, *Leaves from the Notebooks of a Tamed Cynic* (1929; New York: World Publishing Company, Meridian Books, 1960), p. 21; p. 216.
12. W. E. Sangster, *The Approach to Preaching* (Philadelphia: The Westminster Press, 1952), p. 59.

CHAPTER III: CREATIVE EXEGESIS

1. Niebuhr, *Notebooks*, p. 166.
2. James Cox describes the "plain style sermon" in *A Guide to Biblical Preaching* (Nashville: Abingdon, 1976), p. 23.
3. Robert D. Young, *Religious Imagination: God's Gift to Prophets and Preachers* (Philadelphia: The Westminster Press, 1979), p. 34.
4. Leander Keck, *The Bible in the Pulpit: The Renewal of Biblical Preaching* (Nashville: Abingdon, 1978), p. 59.
5. Paul Scherer, *The Word God Sent* (New York: Harper & Row, 1965), p. 26.
6. As quoted by J. H. Jowett, *The Passion for Souls* (New York: Grosset and Dunlap, 1905), p. 59.
7. Sangster, *Approach to Preaching*, p. 81.

CHAPTER IV: TEXT, SERMON FORM, AND CONGREGATIONAL IDENTIFICATION

1. All sermons are from James W. Cox, ed., *Twentieth-Century Pulpit* (Nashville: Abingdon, 1978), pp. 75-81; 42-49; 57-63; 9-14; 115-23; 197-201.
2. James Sanders, *God Has a Story Too: Sermons in Context* (Philadelphia: Fortress Press, 1979).
3. Colin Morris, *The Word and the Words* (Nashville: Abingdon Press, 1975), p. 121.
4. Cox, *Twentieth-Century Pulpit*, pp. 64-74.
5. Gerard Manley Hopkins.
6. Cox, *Twentieth-Century Pulpit*, pp. 20-29.

CHAPTER V: EXPERIMENTAL SERMON FORMS

1. Reported by William D. Thompson and Gordon C. Bennett in *Dialogue Preaching: The Shared Sermon* (Valley Forge, Pa.: Judson Press, 1969).
2. Morris, *Word and the Words*, p. 95.
3. Henry Mitchell, *The Recovery of Preaching* (New York: Harper & Row, 1977), p. 134.
4. I am indebted to Thompson and Bennett, *Dialogue Preaching*, for much of this discussion.
5. *Ibid.*
6. Cox, *Twentieth-Century Pulpit*, pp. 214-19; 141-52.
7. *Ibid.*, pp. 50-56; 108-14.
8. April 1976, p. 6.

9. William Holladay, *Isaiah: Scroll of a Prophetic Heritage* (Grand Rapids: Eerdmans Publishing Company, 1978), pp. 225ff.

CHAPTER VI: LOGIC AND STYLE

1. Cox, *Twentieth-Century Pulpit*, pp. 188-96; 226-36.
2. By the author.
3. Quoted by H. H. Farmer in *The Servant of the Word* (Philadelphia: Fortress Press, 1942), p. 50.
4. James Stewart, *Heralds of God* (1946; reprinted Grand Rapids: Baker Book House, 1972), p. 77.
5. By the author.
6. By the author.
7. Adams, *Sense Appeal in Sermons*, pp. 20, 24-26.
8. Cox, *Twentieth-Century Pulpit*, pp. 226-36.

CHAPTER VII: THE USE AND ABUSE OF ILLUSTRATIONS

1. Cox, *Twentieth-Century Pulpit*.
2. D. M. Lloyd-Jones, *Walking with the Giants: A Minister's Guide to Good Reading and Great Preaching* (Grand Rapids: Baker Book House, 1976).
3. Cox, *Twentieth-Century Pulpit*, pp. 99-107.
4. By the author.
5. *Newsweek*, December 20, 1976, p. 60.
6. Stewart, *A Faith to Proclaim* (Grand Rapids: Baker Book House, 1972), pp. 65-66.

FOR FURTHER READING

Achtemeier, Elizabeth. *The Old Testament and the Proclamation of the Gospel*. Philadelphia: The Westminster Press, 1973.

Beardslee, William A. *Literary Criticism of the New Testament*. Guides to Biblical Scholarship; New Testament Series, edited by Dan O. Via, Jr. Philadelphia: Fortress Press, 1970.

Best, Ernest. *From Text to Sermon: Responsible Use of the New Testament in Preaching*. Atlanta: John Knox Press, 1978.

Buechner, Frederick. *Telling the Truth: The Gospel as Tragedy, Comedy, and Fairy Tale*. New York: Harper & Row, 1977.

Craddock, Fred B. *Overhearing the Gospel*. Nashville: Abingdon, 1978.

Keck, Leander E. *The Bible in the Pulpit:The Renewal of Biblical Preaching*. Nashville: Abingdon, 1978.

Knoche, H. Gerard. *The Creative Task: Writing the Sermon*. The Preacher's Workshop Series, book 5. St. Louis: Concordia Publishing House, 1977.

Rorhbaugh, Richard L. *The Biblical Interpreter*. Philadelphia: Fortress Press, 1978.

Sanders, James A. *God Has a Story Too: Sermons in Context*. Philadelphia: Fortress Press, 1979.

Thielicke, Helmut. *Encounter with Spurgeon*. Translated by John W. Doberstein. Grand Rapids: Baker Book House, 1975.

von Rad, Gerhard. *Biblical Interpretations in Preaching*. Translated by John E. Steely. Nashville: Abingdon, 1977.

Wilder, Amos N. *The Language of the Gospel: Early Christian Rhetoric*. New York: Harper & Row, 1964.

INDEX